AIR POLLUTION INDICES

A Compendium and Assessment of
Indices Used in the United States and Canada

GARY C. THOM 2736913

Consultant to the President's Council on
Environmental Quality
Washington, D.C.

and

WAYNE R. OTT

Monitoring Technology Division
Office of Research and Development
U.S. Environmental Protection Agency
Washington, D.C.

This original publication was sponsored by
The President's Council on Environmental Quality
and the U.S. Environmental Protection Agency

ANN ARBOR SCIENCE
PUBLISHERS INC
P.O. BOX 1425 • ANN ARBOR, MICH. 48106

Published 1976 by Ann Arbor Science Publishers, Inc.
P.O. Box 1425, Ann Arbor, Michigan 48106

Library of Congress Catalog Card Number 76-41114
ISBN 0-250-40148-7

The original publication was sponsored by The
President's Council on Environmental Quality and
the U.S. Environmental Protection Agency,
December 1975.

FOREWORD

The American public needs to be provided with accurate, timely, and understandable information about air quality conditions in the nation's cities. Awareness of the daily level of urban air pollution is often important to those who suffer from illnesses which are aggravated or caused by air pollution, as well as to the general public. Many Americans who live or work in urban areas can voluntarily modify their activities at times when they are cognizant of high air pollution levels. Further, the success of the nation's commitment to improving air quality may depend upon the support of citizens who are well-informed about local and nation-wide air pollution problems and the progress of abatement efforts.

In recent years, dozens of states and municipalities throughout the United States and Canada have responded to these public information needs by developing or adopting various kinds of air pollution indices for daily reporting. The news media have widely adopted these indices, and the result has been that most of the air quality information now provided to the general public is communicated in the form of an air quality index. Thus, there now exists a wealth of experience in using air pollution indices for public reporting.

This report draws upon that experience to summarize and assess the many air pollution indices that are regularly being used to communicate air quality information to citizens of the United States and Canada. The first comprehensive study of its kind, this compendium and assessment was performed by Gary C. Thom, a consultant to the Council on Environmental Quality, and Wayne R. Ott of the U.S. Environmental Protection Agency's Office of Research and Development. The study was conducted in response to recent recommendations of the National Academy of Sciences and the Congressional Research Service that CEQ, EPA, and other Federal agencies should increase the efforts devoted to developing and utilizing better air quality indicators for public information. The contributions of many state and municipal agency personnel were invaluable to the success of the study.

The findings of this study are quite disturbing. The report describes a confusing and scientifically inconsistent array of air quality reporting methods in use today. At least 15 basically different kinds of indices are used, and few of them seem to provide truly meaningful information to the public.

As a result of this study, the Council on Environmental Quality established a Federal Interagency Task Force on Air Quality Indicators in the summer of 1975. The primary mission of the task force is to develop a standard air pollution index which the participating Federal agencies can recommend for nationwide use. The task force consists of CEQ, the U.S. Environmental Protection Agency, and the National Bureau of Standards, the National Oceanic and Atmospheric Administration, and the Office of Environmental Affairs of the Department of Commerce.

Appendices E and F of this report describe two of the air pollution indices which are being actively considered by the task force: the Standardized Urban Air Quality Index and the Primary Standards Index. Although neither of these indices has yet received the endorsement of the task force, both of them were developed by CEQ and EPA personnel who were cognizant of the findings of this compendium and assessment of U.S. and Canadian air pollution indices. It is expected that some of the design features of both of these candidate indices will become incorporated into a Standard Air Pollution Index which will be recommended by the task force. The task force expects to report its recommendations in the spring of 1976.

Russell W. Peterson, Chairman
Council on Environmental Quality

ABSTRACT

This report presents the findings of a detailed survey of air pollution indices that are presently utilized or available. The survey included a review of the existing literature on air pollution indices, telephone discussions with personnel from the 55 largest air pollution control agencies in the United States and Canada, and a case study of a three-State region in which an attempt is being made to develop a uniform air pollution index. These three data sources have enabled the preparation of the most extensive compendium of air pollution index material currently in existence.

Two general types of air pollution indices have been developed: (1) short-term and (2) long-term. This study provides the first systematic analysis of the short-term indices that are used routinely by local agencies and news media across the Nation to provide the public with simple guides for assessing the severity of local air pollution. Of the 55 metropolitan air pollution control agencies surveyed in the United States, 33 routinely used some form of short-term air quality index. However, it was found that nearly all of the indices had different mathematical formulations and different meanings to the public. For example, an index value of 100 reported in Washington, D.C., meant something entirely different from a value of 100 reported in Cleveland, Ohio. The long-term indices, which indicate trends in environmental quality, are intended primarily for use in formulating and evaluating local or national environmental policies. As a result, virtually none of the long-term indices are being used by metropolitan air pollution control agencies.

The diversity of air pollution indices creates potential confusion, raises questions about their technical validity, and prevents the indices from being used to give a national picture of air pollution problems. From the case study and agency comments, it was possible to identify general criteria which would need to be met by a standardized index. These criteria were then used to formulate two examples of possible standardized air quality indices. To evaluate the feasibility of establishing a standardized index, it is recommended that a Federal Interagency Task Force on Air Pollution Indicators be established.

TABLE OF CONTENTS

LIST OF TABLES

LIST OF TABLES (Cont'd)

LIST OF FIGURES

CHAPTER I

EXECUTIVE SUMMARY

1. Purpose of Study

Public awareness of air pollution problems has increased the need for timely information about changes in air pollution levels. Every day, air quality conditions in our Nation's cities are presently being reported to millions of Americans by local agencies and news media. In more than half of our large cities, the public receives this information -- on television, on the radio, and in print -- through the use of various air pollution indices. A typical air pollution index is an interpretive technique which transforms complex data on measured atmospheric pollutant concentrations into a single number or set of numbers in order to make the data more understandable.

Although many technical papers proposing specific indices appear in the literature, no detailed study has been available to describe the characteristics of the many indices that are actually being used for public reporting. How many air pollution indices are there in the United States? What are the experiences of metropolitan agencies with these indices? Have the indices proposed in the literature been adopted by State and local air pollution control agencies? What pollutants do the indices include? How are the indices calculated and how are the individual pollutants weighted? What reporting formats are used to convey this information to the public?

This study is the first comprehensive effort of its kind designed to answer these questions by assembling a national inventory of the air pollution indices currently in existence. It draws upon this inventory to compare different indices, to make inferences about current practices regarding these indices, and to identify relevant problems that should be brought to the attention of public officials.

2. Methodology

This study employed three main approaches to gather information: (1) a review of the existing literature on air pollution indices; (2) a survey soliciting information from air pollution control agencies in U.S. cities, States, and Canadian Provinces; and (3) a case study of a three-State area in which an attempt is being made to adopt a uniform air quality index. The information for the survey was solicited by telephoning the 55 largest metropolitan (city and county) air pollution control agencies in the United States, as well as a number of

State and Province agencies that make use of indices.

The case study of the Steubenville-Wheeling-Pittsburgh

(three-State) area provided information about the problems

encountered when three neighboring jurisdictions, each of

which presently uses a different index, attempt to adopt a

common format.

An extensive library of documentation of air pollution

indices was developed during this study. This report

presents a systematic analysis of the data contained in

this documentation.

3. Findings

This study has revealed a great diversity and lack of

consistency in the way air quality conditions are reported to

the public by means of air pollution indices. States,

Provinces, and U.S. cities use daily informational indices

which differ from each other and which greatly differ from

the more complex, long-term trend indices that appear in

the scientific literature. State and local air pollution

control agencies clearly prefer the simpler types of indices.

Nevertheless, the variation in these simpler indices is

striking. Among the 33 United States cities and five States

currently utilizing daily air pollution indices, there are
15 basically different index types. With two minor exceptions
(when the descriptor categories* are taken into account), <u>no</u>
<u>two indices are the same</u>. This diversity suggests that
consistent scientific rationales have been lacking in the
development of air quality indices.

Because of this variability, the individual who travels
to different cities may easily become confused about air
pollution levels in each city. The table on the following
page illustrates this problem. In 13 cities, a reported
index value of 25 (or 25 ppm for carbon monoxide) would be
accompanied by any of 10 different descriptor words. If a
citizen does not differentiate between index types, he
would encounter descriptor words in different cities
ranging from "unhealthy" to "fair" to "excellent," all
describing the same index value of 25. Striking differences also are found in the way different cities calculate
their indices, the number of pollutants they include, and
the manner in which they report their indices to the public.
To quantitatively summarize these differences, the authors
of this study developed an index classification system.

---

*A "descriptor category" is the interpretive word
issued along with the index value (for example, "good",
"unhealthy", "clean air").

4

HOW 13 CITIES REPORT AN INDEX VALUE OF 25[a]

City	Calculation Method[b]	Air Pollution Descriptor
Tampa, FL	A	Moderate
Denver, CO	B	Fair
Washington, DC	B	Fair
Baltimore, MD	B	Fair
Cincinnati, OH	B	Excellent
Miami, FL	C	Normal
Louisville, KY	C	Good
Los Angeles, CA	D	Stage 1
San Francisco, CA	D	Severe
St. Paul, MN	D	Unhealthy
Trenton, NJ	D	Unsatisfactory
Albany, NY	D	High
New York, NY	D	Unhealthy

[a] For methods A, B, and C the index value of I=25 is calculated from one or more pollutant concentrations; for method D, individual pollutant concentrations are reported and an index value of 25 corresponds to 25 ppm carbon monoxide.

[b] The calculation method is the most important component of the index type; see Chapter VI for further explanation.

The present diversity of air pollution indices creates
potential confusion, raises questions of technical validity,
and prevents the indices from being used by anyone to obtain
a national indication of air pollution problems. From the
comments received from air pollution control agency personnel,
it is evident that a standard air pollution index, or
a standardized air quality reporting format, might be both
beneficial and welcome. However, as seen in the three-State
case study, a standardization effort is an extremely difficult and complex undertaking. From the case study and
agency comments, it was possible to identify general criteria
which would need to be met by any standardized index. Based
on these criteria, two examples are given of possible
standardized indices (Appendices E and F). Such a standardization effort also should specify the ways in which a
local agency might select the data for the index, including
quality control practices, instrumentation, and site location
criteria.

4.   Recommendation

To evaluate the feasibility of establishing a standardized
index and standardized index monitoring criteria, it is
recommended that a Federal Interagency Task Force on Air

6

Quality Indicators be established. This report should serve

as the starting point for the deliberations of this task force.

The task force also should consider the development of an

Index Monitoring Guidelines document to assist local agencies

that wish to adopt such a standardized index system or

reporting format.

CHAPTER II

SUMMARY OF FINDINGS

This study has revealed great diversity and lack of consistency in the air pollution indices that are currently used by air pollution control agencies in the United States and Canada. Of the 55 largest U.S. metropolitan air pollution control agencies surveyed in this study (those with more than 10 staff members), 33 use an air pollution index. Five States and two Canadian Provinces operate State-wide (or Province-wide) index systems. Most of these indices have been initiated since 1970.

No strong relationship emerges between the size of an agency and its tendency to use or not use an air pollution index. Small agencies (fewer than 20 staff members) appear less likely to use indices, perhaps because they lack the monitoring data or the staff to routinely compute an index.

By developing an "index classification system," it was possible to analyze and compare the various indices reported in the literature and those that are used by the agencies surveyed. For each index, this system evaluated:

- Number of variables

- Calculation method and mode

- Descriptor categories

The majority of the indices appearing <u>in the literature</u>
incorporate five of the six National Ambient Air Quality
Standards (NAAQS) pollutants (excluding hydrocarbons), use
a nonlinear calculation method, and combine variables into
one number (combined mode) rather than reporting them
separately. The descriptor categories for these indices
are either arbitrary or based on the NAAQS.

The index classification system identified 15 basic
kinds of indices in the city, State, and Provincial agencies.
Among the 33 U.S. cities with indices, 40 percent use indices
of five variables. The remaining agencies are approximately
equally divided among those using one, two, or three variables.
Nearly all of the cities (91 percent) incorporate particulate
matter (total suspended particulates or coefficient of haze,
with the latter twice as common). The next most commonly
used index pollutants are carbon monoxide (73 percent of the
agencies), sulfur dioxide (73 percent), oxidant (52 percent),
and nitrogen dioxide (48 percent). One index includes
visibility and another incorporates particle scattering alone.

A majority of U.S. city agencies (58 percent) favor
a linear calculation method. Approximately one-third

report actual concentration values. Only four agencies (13 percent) use a nonlinear method. Forty percent of the agencies base their index on the maximum of one of the variables it contains, while 33 percent report all variables individually. Only 27 percent aggregate the variables together into a combined index. Although most agencies prefer either three or four descriptor categories, a total of 41 different descriptor words are identified. The majority of the U.S. agencies (67 percent) base their descriptor categories either on the NAAQS or on the recommended Federal Episode Criteria; the remainder use arbitrary categories.

The State-wide and regional index systems (Minnesota, New Jersey, New York, Ohio, and the District of Columbia metropolitan area) incorporate three, four, or five variables into their index. Two of these systems report actual concentrations; two use a linear function; and one reports actual concentrations along with a nonlinear index. As in the cities, three or four descriptor categories are preferred, although one State system uses 12 categories. All State systems base their categories on the NAAQS or the Federal Episode Criteria.

Table 1 summarizes the findings of this report by comparing the characteristics of the indices appearing in the literature with those used by U.S. cities, States, and Canadian Provinces. Very striking differences emerge, particularly when indices in the literature are compared with those in current use by air pollution control agencies. Most published indices are relatively complex: they employ a nonlinear calculation method and are combined in form. Although the two Canadian Provinces use this type of index, the U.S. State and city indices prefer the simpler linear calculation methods and seldom combine variables. Thus, the air pollution indices which have been formally proposed or discussed in the literature are not widely used by U.S. air pollution control agencies.

Some insight into why this may be so is provided by the comments from air pollution agency personnel (Chapter VI). One reason for an agency choosing a simple index, or, in some cases, choosing no index at all, is the need for the index values to be consistent with the public's perception of air pollution levels (reduced visibility, eye irritation, etc.). Many of the published indices do not address this problem.

TABLE 1

DIFFERENCES IN THE DESIGN CHARACTERISTICS OF VARIOUS INDICES

Indices (Sample size)	Number of Pollutant Variables Included		Calculation Method and Mode					Descriptor Basis	
	1 - 3	4 - 6	Nonlinear	Linear [a/]	Actual Concentrations	Combined	Uncombined [b/]	Standards and Episode Criteria	Arbitrary
Indices Appearing in the Literature (8)	37%	63% [d/]	63%	37%	-	88%	12%	50%	50%
Indices in Use (40) [c/]	52%	48%	18%	52%	30%	30%	70%	70%	30%
U.S. Cities (33) [c/]	54%	46%	12%	58%	30%	27%	73%	67%	33%
U.S. States (5) [c/]	40%	60%	20%	40%	40%	20%	80%	100%	-
Canadian Provinces (2)	50%	50%	100%	-	-	100%	-	50%	50%

a/ Includes both linear with nonconstant coefficients and linear with constant coefficients (see Table 13).

b/ Includes individual and maximum modes (see Chapter VI).

c/ Does not include adjustments for agencies which use two calculation methods (see Tables 13 and 14).

d/ Pindex includes seven variables.

As part of this investigation, a case study also was conducted in a three-State region attempting to adopt a common air pollution index. Although many problems arise from such a multijurisdictional effort, there was general agreement -- also observed in the comments from some U.S. Federal agencies -- that confusion could be reduced if the Federal Government were to develop, endorse, and support a single, uniform air pollution index. From the study results, it is evident that the following criteria would be desirable in any standardized index:

- Easily understood by the public

- Not inconsistent with perceived air pollution levels

- Spatially meaningful

- Includes major pollutants (and able to include future pollutants)

- Calculated in a simple manner using reasonable assumptions

- Rests on a reasonable scientific basis

- Relates to ambient air quality standards and goals

- Relates to episode criteria

- Exhibits day-to-day variation

- Can be forecast a day in advance

As part of this study, two examples of possible standardized indices have been developed and are offered for consideration (Appendices E and F).

CHAPTER III

INTRODUCTION

In this era of "social indicators," combining the
many parameters that provide measures of air pollution
into one number is an appealing prospect. Certainly, one
number that could accurately indicate the "severity" of
air pollution in a given city or across the Nation would be
of use both to the general public and to those involved in
implementation of air pollution control policies. While
this goal appears worthwhile, achieving it is not simple.
The complexity of the air pollution problem makes it
difficult to develop an index that is really meaningful.

To see how different air pollution control agencies
have approached this problem, the 55 largest metropolitan
air pollution control agencies in the United States were
surveyed in-depth. Canadian Provincial agencies and State
air pollution control agencies in the United States known to
use air pollution indices were also surveyed. In addition,
the literature was reviewed at length to determine the
characteristics of published air pollution indices and the
experiences with these indices of persons engaged in research

or administration. Finally, a case study was undertaken of three neighboring United States cities which were attempting to develop a common air pollution index.

1. <u>Definition of Index</u>

An "air pollution index" is defined in this study as a scheme that transforms the (weighted) values of individual air pollution-related parameters (for example, carbon monoxide concentration or visibility) into a single number, or set of numbers (Figure 1).* The result is

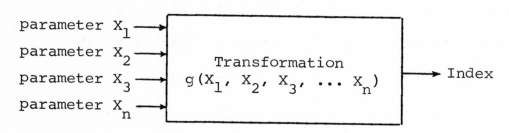

parameter X_1 →

parameter X_2 →

parameter X_3 →

parameter X_n →

Transformation
$g(X_1, X_2, X_3, \ldots X_n)$

→ Index

Figure 1. Index calculation

a set of rules (for example, an equation) that translates parameter values -- by means of a numerical manipulation -- into a more parsimonious form. (In <u>set</u> <u>theory</u>, this process

<hr>

*Some other recent publications, such as those of the Council on Environmental Quality[1] and the National Academy of Sciences,[2] have defined indices more broadly to include, for example, air, water, and recreation. Such a broad definition was not suitable for the scope of this investigation.

is viewed as mapping of elements contained in one sample
space into another sample space.)

The following evaluations were made to determine
whether an agency used an "index." If an agency reported
just the actual air pollutant concentration values to the
public -- micrograms per cubic meter or parts per million
(ppm) -- or concentration values along with the Federal
standards, this was not considered an "index." Rather,
an index must be based on some set of rules which translate
the values into a new variable, or which make interpretations
of these values. At the very least, an index is any system
in which specific concentrations ranges are grouped into
air quality "descriptor categories." For example, a system
which designates 0-3 ppm carbon monoxide as "good," 3-15 ppm
as "satisfactory," and 15-40 ppm as "unsatisfactory" was
considered to be an index. In its most elaborate form, an
index is an equation which combines many pollutants in some
mathematical expression to arrive at a single number for
air quality.

Air quality indices can be grouped into two categories:

- Long-term indices
- Short-term indices

The long-term indices are intended to evaluate changes in air quality over periods of several years or more. A typical example of such an index is the Mitre Air Quality Index[1,3] which was applied to air quality data for a number of cities across the country. Ideally, these indices are for the purpose of assessing the effectiveness of enforcement polices in improving air quality; however, few are being used in practice. Long-term indices appear often in the literature, as discussed in Chapter IV.

The short-term indices are used widely by State and local air pollution control agencies and are the focal point of this investigation. These indices, which seldom have been described in the literature, usually are intended to inform the public about daily changes in air pollution levels. Although episode warning systems are not reported daily, they do consist of descriptor categories which are reported whenever concentrations exceed specified levels. In some cities, this happens frequently, and the distinction between an episode warning system and a daily informational index becomes blurred. Thus, air pollution agencies with episode warning systems are classified as having indices.

2. Air Quality Standards and Episode Criteria

Many air pollution indices are based on existing
Federal air quality standards, on recommended Federal Episode
Criteria, or on both. The Clean Air Act[5] authorizes the
Federal Government to establish National Ambient Air Quality
Standards (NAAQS) for those air pollutants which are poten-
tially harmful to the public health and welfare. In April
1971, NAAQS were established for six air pollutants: sulfur
dioxide (SO_2); particulate matter (total suspended particulate,
TSP); carbon monoxide (CO); photochemical oxidant (principally
ozone, O_3); nitrogen dioxide (NO_2); and nonmethane hydrocarbons.[6] The standard for nonmethane hydrocarbons was
established not because hydrocarbons affect health and welfare
but because they are a precursor to oxidant in the atmosphere;
they are therefore controlled to achieve the oxidant standard.
The NAAQS (Table 2) are not to be exceeded more than once a
year. Primary standards are intended to protect against
adverse effects on human health, while secondary standards
are intended to protect against effects on welfare (effects
on vegetation, materials, visibility, etc.). For some
pollutants, both one-year and shorter-term values (1, 3, 8,
or 24 hours) are specified.

TABLE 2

NATIONAL AMBIENT AIR QUALITY STANDARDS
AND
RECOMMENDED FEDERAL EPISODE CRITERIA

Pollutant, Units/ Averaging Time	Secondary	Primary	Alert[a]	Warning[a]	Emergency[a]	Significant Harm[b]
Sulfur dioxide $\mu g/m^3$ (ppm)						
1 year		80(0.03)				
24 hours		365(0.14)	800(0.3)	1,600(0.6)	2,100(0.8)	2,620(1.0)
3 hours	1,300(0.5)					
Particulate matter $\mu g/m^3$ (COH)						
1 year	60	75				
24 hours	150	260	375(3.0)	625(5.0)	875(7.0)	1,000(8.0)
Product of sulfur dioxide and particulate matter $[\mu g/m^3]^2$ (ppm x COH)			6.5×10^4 (0.2)	2.61×10^5 (0.8)	3.93×10^5 (1.2)	4.90×10^5 (1.5)
Carbon monoxide mg/m^3 (ppm)						
8 hours	10(9)	10(9)	17(15)	34(30)	46(40)	57.5(50)
1 hour	40(35)	40(35)				144(125)
Oxidants $\mu g/m^3$ (ppm)						
1 hour	160(0.08)	160(0.08)	200(0.1)	800(0.4)	1,000(0.5)	1,200(0.6)
Nitrogen dioxide $\mu g/m^3$ (ppm)						
1 year	100(0.05)	100(0.05)				
24 hours			282(0.15)	565(0.3)	750(0.4)	938(0.5)
1 hour			1,130(0.6)	2,260(1.2)	3,000(1.6)	3,750(2.0)
Hydrocarbons $\mu g/m^3$ (ppm) 3 hours (6 to 9 a.m.)	160(0.24)	160(0.24)				

[a] The Federal Episode Criteria specify that meteorological conditions are such that pollutant concentrations can be expected to remain at these levels for twelve (12) or more hours or increase; or, in the case of oxidants, the situation is likely to reoccur within the next 24 hours unless control actions are taken.

[b] Priority 1 regions must have a contingency plan which shall, as a minimum, provide for taking any emission control actions necessary to prevent ambient pollutant concentration at any location from reaching these levels.

The States are required to develop emergency episode plans for regions designated by the Federal Government as "Priority I Regions." The Federal Government has published "example regulations"[7] which are intended as guidelines to assist the States in developing episode plans. These example regulations include recommended "Episode Criteria" specifying concentration values which "justify the proclamation of an air pollution alert, air pollution warning, or air pollution emergency." The criteria include values for all pollutants covered by the NAAQS except hydrocarbons (Table 2). Using the Federal Episode Criteria, an air pollution control agency would declare an "Alert", the first stage of the episode warning system, whenever the specified concentration for any one of the five air pollutants is reached or exceeded at any air monitoring site. The Federal Episode Criteria also include specified values for the product of sulfur dioxide and particulate matter.

Two different measurement techniques are commonly used for particulate matter -- the high-volume sampler and the tape sampler. The high-volume sampler gives the 24-hour average of TSP in micrograms per cubic meter, while the tape sampler gives coefficient-of-haze (COH) units for averaging periods as short as 2 hours. There is considerable evidence that the two measurement techniques do not provide compatible results, and the Federal Government has specified the high-volume sampler as the "standard reference method" for use by the States in determining compliance with the particulate NAAQS. In this report, TSP denotes particulate matter as measured by the high-volume sampler, while COH refers to the tape sampler measurement.

CHAPTER IV

LITERATURE REVIEW

The literature on air pollution indices[8-18] has focused on the development of long-term trend indices. Little has been published on the short-term indices commonly used by State and local air pollution agencies. Although the long-term indices have appeared in the literature, discussions with governmental personnel have revealed few cases in which such indices have actually been used to develop or evaluate major air pollution policies.

Each of the eight air pollution indices reported in the literature (Table 3) differs in terms of the number of applicable pollutants, method of index calculation, and descriptor categories. As a result, the overall meaning of each index is different. One of the first short-term air quality indices to be published was Green's Index.[8] This index, which combines subindices for sulfur dioxide and smoke shade (COH), is based on proposed and adopted air quality standards and on projected concentration/health effects relationships. The coefficients and exponents for

Table 3
AIR POLLUTION INDICES REPORTED IN THE LITERATURE

Name	Variables	Equation	Range	Categories		Description	Reference
Green's Combined Index (CI)	SO_2, COH	$CI = 0.5\,(84.0\,SO_2^{0.431} + 26.6\,COH^{0.576})$	0 - 100+	0-49 50-59 60-69 68+ 100+	Desired level, clean, safe air First alert, intermediate Second alert Third alert Extreme level	Index is based on proposed and adopted air quality standards; SO_2 concentrations for each category differ by a factor of 5.0; COH values differ by a factor of 3.33. Index is applicable only during colder seasons when SO_2 concentrations are elevated.	8
Ontario Air Pollution Index (API)	SO_2, COH	$API = 0.2\,(30.5\,COH + 126.0\,SO_2)^{1.35}$	0 - 580+	0-31 32-49 50-74 75-99 100+	Acceptable Advisory Level First Alert Second Alert Episode Threshold Level	The coefficients and exponent relate API values to pollution levels attained during past air pollution episodes.	9
PINDEX	CO, SO_x, TSP, NO_x, OX, HC	$PINDEX = \dfrac{TSP}{375} + \dfrac{SO_x}{1430} + \dfrac{NO_x}{514} + \dfrac{CO}{40000} + \dfrac{HC}{19300} + \dfrac{OX}{214} + SYN$ where $SYN = PM \cdot SO_x$ synergistic term	0 - 100+	N.A.		Actual pollutant concentrations are divided by their respective tolerance factor (one-hour equivalent standard) which is based on the California or other appropriate standards. The OX value includes that estimated from NO_x + HC + hr $\rightarrow$ OX. The SYN term is the smallest of the PM or SO_x terms.	11
Oak Ridge Air Quality Index (ORAQI)	CO, SO_x, TSP, NO_2, OX	$ORAQI = \left[5.7\sum_i (C_i/S_i)\right]^{1.37}$ C_i = conc. of pollutant i S_i = standard for pollutant i	0 - 1000	-20 20-39 40-59 60-79 80-99 100+	Excellent Good Fair Poor Bad Dangerous	Index may be calculated for any combination of from $i = 1$ to 5 pollutants using nomograph; pollutant standards, S_i, are 24 hr. extrapolations of secondary NAAQS. When pollutant concentrations are at background levels, ORAQI = 10; when all concentrations are at standards, ORAQI = 100.	12
Mitre Air Quality Index (MAQI)	CO, SO_2, TSP, NO_2, OX	$MAQI = \sqrt{\sum_i I_i^2}$ I_i = indicator for each pollutant i	0 - 3+	MAQI < 1: no std. exceeded 1 < MAQI < 3: stds met or exceeded MAQI > 3: one or more std exceeded		Index may be calculated for any combination of $i = 1$ to 5 pollutants; indicator, I_i, is based on secondary NAAQS: $$I_i = \sqrt{\left(\frac{C_{ia}}{S_{ia}}\right)^2 + h\sum_i \left(\frac{C_{ih}}{S_{ih}}\right)^2}$$ where: C_{ia} = mean concentration of pollutant i, during longest measurement period a, as specified by standard S_{ia}. C_{ih} = mean concentration of pollutant i, during hourly measurement period h, as specified by standard S_{ih}. $h = 1$ if $C_{ih} > S_{ih}$. $h = 0$ if $C_{ih} < S_{ih}$.	3
Extreme Value Index (EVI)	CO, SO_2, TSP, OX	$EVI = \sqrt{\sum_i E_i^2}$ E_i = indicator for each pollutant i	0, -1	EVI = 0: all stds being met EVI = 1: at least one std exceeded		Index may be calculated for any combination of $i = 1$ to 4 pollutants; E_i is based on those secondary NAAQS not to be exceeded more than once per year, e.g., the hourly stds and is given by: $$E_i = \sqrt{\sum_i \left(\frac{A_{ih}}{S_{ih}}\right)^2}; \quad A_{ih} = \sum_j h_j\,(C_{ih})_j$$ where: A_{ih} = summation of those values, C_{ih}, which exceed the hourly measurement period h, for pollutant i, as specified by standard S_{ih}. $h_j = 1$ if $(C_{ih})_j > S_{ih}$ $h_j = 0$ if $(C_{ih})_j < S_{ih}$	3
Combustion Products Index (CPI)	N.A.	$CPI = \dfrac{\text{Fuel Burned}}{\text{Ventilating Volume}}$	N.A.	N.A.		The fuel burned (tons) is obtained by inventorying fuel deliveries; ventilating volume (volume of air into which the fuel combustion products are mixed) is the product of the inventory area, mixing depth, and wind speed.	14
Air Quality Index (AQI)	CO, SO_2, TSP, NO_2, OX	$AQI = \sum_i W_i PI_i$ W_i = weighting factor for pollutant severity PI_i = standardized pollutant index	N.A. N.A.	N.A. N.A.		The AQI may be calculated for any combination of from $i = 1$ to 5 pollutants whose concentrations are predicted by a simple diffusion model using emission inventory data; the predicted concentrations are then standardized to give the standardized pollutant index, PI_i: $$PI_i = \bar{Y} + \frac{S\,(X_i - \bar{X}_i)}{s_i}$$ where: $\bar{Y}$ = preset mean S = preset standard deviation X_i = predicted pollutant concentration $\bar{X}_i$ = mean predicted pollutant concentration s_i = standard deviation of predicted pollutant concentrations	13

the sulfur dioxide and COH index equations were chosen so
that the resulting values fit pre-selected categories. The
combined index value then is obtained by averaging the two
subindices. [Ontario[9-10] uses a similar index (Appendix B),
with the coefficients and exponents changed slightly to fit
air quality standards in effect in Canada.] Green's index,
exhibits what may be termed an "eclipsing" phenomenon.
Eclipsing occurs because one of the several pollutant
concentrations in the index can exceed its air quality
standard, but the combined index value can simultaneously
be less than a value equivalent to the standard. Eclipsing
is characteristic of many combined indices.

The Pindex equation[11] combines the weighted concentrations of the six NAAQS pollutants with terms representing
solar radiation and the particulate-sulfur oxides synergism.
The weighting factors are based on the 1-hour equivalent[*]
of the California standards proposed when the index was
developed. The Pindex equation may be applied to long-term
ambient air quality data or to emission data from specific

---

[*]The 1-hour equivalent concentrations are obtained by
a correlation analysis relating the 1-hour and 24-hour
average concentrations.

source categories such as transportation, industry, power plants, space heating, and refuse combustion. As a combined pollutant index, Pindex exhibits an eclipsing effect.

The Oak Ridge Air Quality Index[12/] is based on the 1-hour equivalent concentrations of the secondary NAAQS. It is calculated for any combination of from one to five of the pollutants using a specially designed nomograph. The co-efficient and exponent of this index have been selected to give index values of 10 at background pollution levels and 100 when pollutant concentrations exceed the standards. Although the range is divided into several well-defined categories, no correlation with health effects is implied by its developers.

The Mitre Air Quality Index[3/] (MAQI) is based on the secondary NAAQS and is intended to depict quarterly changes in air quality, using data for the most recent 12-month period. The index is calculated as the square root of the sum of squares of five of the six NAAQS pollutants (excluding hydrocarbons). Each component, in turn, is the square root of the sum of squares of the normalized pollutant concentrations. These normalized pollutant concentrations are obtained by dividing the mean pollutant concentration by the standard applicable to the averaging time.

Although this method of calculation guarantees an index value of at least 1.0 if any pollutant included in the computation exceeds its standard value, it introduces a gray area between 1.0 and 3.0 where each pollutant concentration may or may not exceed its standard. When index values occur in this range, each indicator is inspected to determine if a standard has been exceeded. Values greater than 3.0 imply that at least one standard has been exceeded. The purpose of the δ coefficient in the indicator equation is to eliminate from the index calculation pollutant concentrations below their respective standards. This feature prevents eclipsing.

The Extreme Value Index[3] (EVI) is calculated in a fashion similar to the MAQI except that the EVI indicators sum only those squares of the pollutant/standard ratios which are greater than or equal to 1.0. Such a calculation scheme (which avoids the eclipsing phenomenon) measures the extent of very high-level pollution for short periods of time and therefore can be used to describe episodes. The resulting index range is discontinuous between 0.0 and 1.0, with values greater than 1.0 indicating that standards are being exceeded.

CHAPTER V

SURVEY DESIGN

The existing air pollution literature can provide little information about the routine use of indices by air pollution control agencies. To learn which air pollution indices are in common use and to gain insight into the experiences of air pollution control agencies with these indices, an in-depth survey of these agencies was required. In this survey, agencies throughout the United States and Canada were telephoned and asked to send information describing their index. The data base in this investigation was assembled from notes taken during the telephone conversations, from written materials received from the agencies, and from a case study involving three neighboring air pollution agencies in Ohio, Pennsylvania, and West Virginia (Chapter VII).

1. Survey Population

The population surveyed in this investigation consisted of the 55 largest metropolitan (city and county) air pollution control agencies in the United States, along with State air pollution agencies in the United States known to operate State-wide air pollution index systems.

28

It also included the Canadian Provinces with air pollution control agency staffs of 10 or more persons and one Canadian city which uses an index. To select the survey population, the total number of staff members from every city and county air pollution agency was computed using the Directory of Governmental Air Pollution Agencies, published by the Air Pollution Control Association.[19] Only those U.S. air pollution agencies having 10 or more staff members were included in this survey population (Table 4). In the United States, the resulting survey population consisted of 55 agencies. Telephone inquiries revealed that, in 14 of these cities, the index was operated as part of a general State-wide or regional index system. Six States were operating this type of system: Connecticut, District of Columbia, New York, New Jersey, Minnesota, and Ohio. These State indices serve 59 cities (Table 5), but many of these air pollution agencies have staffs smaller than 10 persons. Also, the agencies in Baltimore, Maryland, Boston, Massachusetts, and Portland, Oregon, are operated by the State but are not part of a State-wide system. In Portland, the State not only reports the air pollution index but it operates the entire

TABLE 4

U.S. CITY/COUNTY AIR POLLUTION CONTROL AGENCIES WITH STAFFS GREATER THAN 10

City/County	Agency Size	Material Received	Index In Use	Comments
Birmingham, AL	17	●		
Phoenix, AZ	25			Discontinued Index
Anaheim, CA	24		●	Replaced Index
Los Angeles, CA	380	●	●	Replaced Index
Riverside, CA	26			
San Bernardino, CA	53			
San Diego, CA	53			
San Francisco, CA	220	●	●	Replaced Index
*Denver, CO	54	●	●	
**New Haven, CN	11			Discontinued Index
**Washington, DC	14	●	●	
Bradenton, FL	11			
Jacksonville, FL	15	●	●	
Miami, FL	50	●	●	
Sarasota, FL	21	●	●	
Tampa, FL	16	●	●	
Atlanta, GA	14	●	●	
Chicago, IL	175	●		
Gary, IN	18			
Indianapolis, IN	15			
Louisville, KY	39	●	●	
*Baltimore, MD	90	●	●	Replaced Index
**Montgomery Co., MD	10	●	●	
*Boston, MA	87	●		
Springfield, MA	12			
Detroit, MI	77	●	●	
**St. Paul, MN	13	●	●	
Kansas City, MO	15			
St. Louis, MO	35			
Albuquerque, NM	15			
**Albany, NY	237		●	
**Buffalo, NY	44	●	●	
**Mineola, NY	37		●	
New York City, NY	382		●	
**Rochester, NY	12		●	
Charlotte, NC	14			
**Akron, OH	13		●	
**Cincinnati, OH	65	●	●	Replaced Index
**Cleveland, OH	80	●	●	
**Dayton, OH	45		●	Replaced Index
**Toledo, OH	25		●	
Oklahoma City, OK	15	●		Discontinued Index
*Portland, OR	20	●	●	
Philadelphia, PA	94	●	●	
Pittsburgh, PA	82	●	●	
Chattanooga, TN	22		●	
Memphis, TN	14		●	
Nashville, TN	17	●	●	
Dallas, TX	21	●	●	
El Paso, TX	10			
Houston, TX	76	●		
Pasadena, TX	45			
**Fairfax Co., VA	12		●	
Seattle, WA	39	●	●	
Milwaukee, WI	25			

* = City index is operated by State but is not part of statewide index system.
** = City index is part of statewide or regional index system.

30

TABLE 5

STATE-WIDE AIR POLLUTION INDEX SYSTEMS

State	Applicable City or County	Agency Size[a]	State	Applicable City or County	Agency Size[a]
Connecticut (Discontinued Index)	Bridgeport	<10	New Jersey (Cont'd.)	Perth Amboy	<10
	Greenwich	<10		Phillipsburg	--
	Hartford	105*		Somerville	--
	Stamford	<10		Toms River	--
				Trenton	170*
District of Columbia	Alexandria, Va.	<10			
	Arlington Co., Va.	<10	New York	Albany	237*
	Fairfax Co., Va.	12		Buffalo	44
	Prince Georges Co., Md.	<10		Kingston	--
	Montgomery Co., Md.	10		Mamaroneck	--
	Washington, D.C.	14*		Mineola-Eisenhower Park	36
				New York City-Roosevelt Isl.	--
Minnesota	Duluth	<10		Niagara Falls	<10
	Minneapolis	37*		Rensselear	<10
	Rochester	<10		Rochester	12
	St. Paul	13		Schenectady	--
				Syracuse	10
New Jersey	Ancora	--		Utica	--
	Asbury Park	--			
	Atlantic City	--	Ohio	Akron	13
	Bayonne	--		Canton	<10
	Burlington	--		Cincinnati	65
	Camden	--		Cleveland	80
	Elizabeth	<10		Columbus	228*
	Freehold	--		Dayton	45
	Hackensack	--		Lorain	<10
	Jersey City	<10		Mansfield	<10
	Morristown	--		Painesville	<10
	Newark	--		Portsmouth	<10
	Paterson	--		Steubenville	<10
	Paulsboro	--		Toledo	25
	Penns Grove	--		Youngstown	<10

a/Where no agency size is given, size is unknown.
*State Agency

31

city air pollution control agency as well. In Baltimore, on the other hand, the State reports the index, but the local air pollution agency is organizationally separate from the State agency.

In Canada, only Montreal operates a city air pollution control agency. Therefore, all Provinces with staffs of 10 or greater were included in the survey population. Alberta and Ontario operate Province-wide air quality indices. Eight cities within these Provinces issue daily indices (Table 6).

TABLE 6

PROVINCE-WIDE AIR POLLUTION INDEX SYSTEMS[a]

Province	Applicable City	Agency Size
Alberta	Calgary	<10
	Edmonton	26*
Ontario	Hamilton	–
	Happy Valley	–
	Sudbury	–
	Toronto	70*
	Welland	–
	Windsor	–

[a]Where no agency size is given, size is unknown.
 *Province agency

32

2. <u>Survey Approach</u>

Telephone calls were made to the agencies in the survey population from August to December 1975. For each agency, a respondent was sought who was very familiar with the agency's air pollution index, if any. In small agencies, this usually turned out to be the agency's director; in the larger agencies, a public information specialist or a professional in the field of monitoring and data analysis usually was the respondent. With the respondent on the telephone, the investigator went through an informal question-and-answer session covering many of the items listed in the "Air Pollution Index Data Sheet" (Appendix A). The diversity and variety of indices prevented the investigators from using a standardized questionnaire form, so the data sheets served only as guides. All respondents contacted were extremely cooperative and enthusiastic about providing information.

Each respondent was asked, "Can you provide any literature or description of your index?" Of the 55 agencies on the major list (Table 4), 28 promised that they would send written materials, and the materials were received from all of these. In some cases, the telephone discussion

provided sufficient information about the index, and no
mailed material was necessary. Some agencies not using
indices provided material that discussed their reasons
for not adopting an index or their experience with a
previously discontinued index.

The findings reported in this study are based mainly
on the large quantity of information mailed in by the
respondents. This information typically covered the nature
of the index, its method of calculation, the history of its
development, and the way in which it is reported. From
this information, along with the notes taken during the
telephone calls, an "Index Analysis Record" was prepared
for each agency (Appendix B). Analysis of these sheets
yielded the quantitative summaries and conclusions in the
following chapters.

3. Case Study

In the telephone survey, it was learned that three
neighboring cities -- Steubenville, Ohio; Pittsburgh,
Pennsylvania; and Wheeling, West Virginia -- were considering
adoption of a common air quality index. Presently, each
jurisdiction uses a different index, and members of the
public are exposed to all three indices through the news

media. This has resulted in confusion about the air quality in each city and in the region as a whole. Adoption of a single index in the tri-State region would alleviate this confusion. Currently, these air pollution agencies are considering how this might be accomplished. Because of the relevance of this effort to the present study, the region was visited several times, and the problem was examined as a case study (Chapter VII).

CHAPTER VI

SURVEY RESULTS

Initially, information from the mailed responses and
from notes taken during each telephone conversation was
condensed and compiled into tables. The tabular compilation
was found to be inadequate, however, due to the varied and
sometimes extensive information received from the agencies.
Consequently, the information was assembled into the three
appendices. An Index Analysis Record (Appendix B) was
developed to present detailed factual information about
each index in a uniform format. Informal comments from the
agencies were copied into an extended table (Appendix C).
Examples of the ways in which indices are reported by the
news media were also recorded (Appendix D).

1. Agencies Using Indices

During the course of the survey, a total of 30 index
systems were reviewed and analyzed (Appendix C). In the
United States, 25 index systems are currently operating and
three have been discontinued. In Canada, two are currently
operating.

Of the 55 United States metropolitan air pollution
control agencies with more than 10 staff members, 33 agencies

(60 percent) currently use an "air pollution index," as defined in Chapter III. The size distribution of the 55 agencies is skewed to the right (Figure 2), with most agencies (60 percent) having fewer than 30 staff members. No clear relationship is apparent between the size of these agencies and their use of indices. However, small agencies (fewer than 20 staff members) are less likely to use indices, either because they do not have sufficient air monitoring data or because they do not have sufficient staff to calculate the index routinely.

Index Variables. The variables included in U.S. city/ county air pollution indices are shown in Table 7. If the soiling index (COH) and high-volume sampler measurements of total suspended particulate (TSP) are lumped together as measures of particulate matter, then particulate becomes the most common air pollutant included by these agencies in their indices. Of these 33 agencies, 30 (91 percent) include either COH or TSP; COH is used by 21 agencies and TSP by 10 (Jacksonville, Florida, uses both). The popularity of these two measures may be due to the increasing use of telemetered air monitoring networks which cannot readily handle TSP data determined by the high volume sampler, and

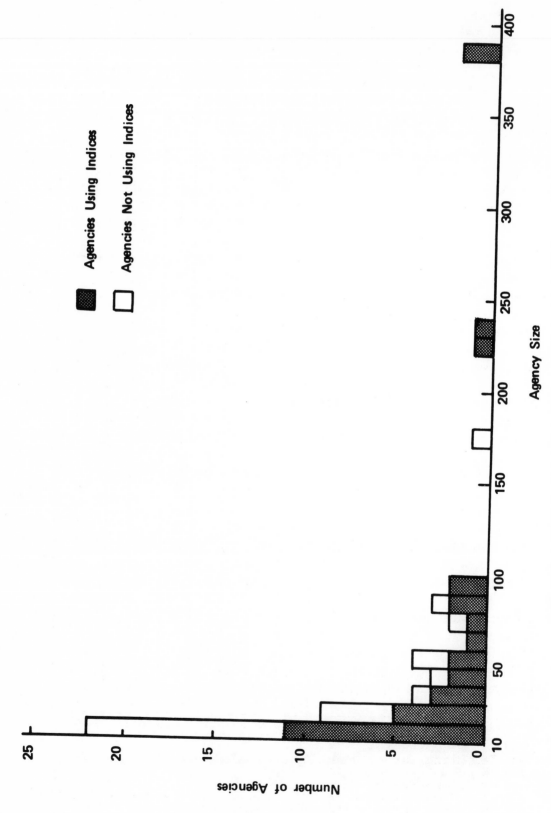

Figure 2.   Size distribution of U.S. city/county air pollution control agencies.

38

TABLE 7

VARIABLES USED IN U.S. CITY/COUNTY AIR POLLUTION INDICES

	Agency Size	CO	SO$_2$	NO$_2$	OX	COH	TSP	VIS	PS	Total
Anaheim, CA	24	•	•		•					3
Los Angeles, CA	380	•	•		•					3
San Francisco, CA	220	•		•	•	•				4
*Denver, CO	54	•				•				2
**Washington, DC	14	•	•	•	•	•				5
Jacksonville, FL	15	•	•	•	•	•	•			6
Miami, FL	50	•		•	•	•		•		5
Tampa, FL	16	•	•	•	•	•				5
Atlanta, GA	14	•	•				•			3
Louisville, KY	39	•	•	•	•	•				5
*Baltimore, MD	90	•	•	•	•	•				5
**Montgomery Co., MD	10	•	•	•	•	•				5
Detroit, MI	77					•				1
**St. Paul, MN	13	•	•				•			3
**Albany, NY	237	•	•			•				3
**Buffalo, NY	44	•	•			•				3
**Mineola, NY	37	•	•			•				3
New York City, NY	382	•	•	•	•	•				5
**Rochester, NY	12	•	•			•				3
**Akron, OH	13	•	•	•	•		•			5
**Cincinnati, OH	65	•	•	•	•		•			5
**Cleveland, OH	80	•	•	•	•		•			5
**Dayton, OH	45	•	•	•	•		•			5
**Toledo, OH	25	•	•	•	•		•			5
*Portland, OR	20								•	1
Philadelphia, PA	94		•			•				2
Pittsburgh, PA	82		•			•				2
Chattanooga, TN	22						•			1
Memphis, TN	14					•				1
Nashville, TN	17					•				1
Dallas, TX	21			•			•			2
**Fairfax Co., VA	12	•	•	•	•	•				5
Seattle, WA	39		•			•				2
TOTAL		24	24	16	17	21	10	1	1	114

COH = Coefficient of Haze
TSP = Total Suspended Particulate (High-volume sampler)
VIS = Visibility
PS = Particle Scattering (Integrating Nephelometer)
 * = City Index is Operated by State but is not Part of State-wide Index System
** = City Index is Part of State-wide or Regional Index System

the shorter averaging time (2-hours) available from the COH tape sampler. CO and SO_2 are the next most common pollutants to be included in these indices -- 24 agencies (73 percent) for each. The next most popular pollutants are oxidant (17 agencies, 52 percent) and NO_2 (16 agencies, 48 percent). Visibility is included in one agency's index, and particle scattering is the only variable making up another agency's index.

When the air pollution indices used by States (or regions) and Canadian Provinces are examined (Table 8), a similar pattern emerges. The most common pollutants are carbon monoxide, sulfur dioxide, and particulates (COH and TSP). The least common pollutant is nitrogen dioxide, with only two agencies -- Ohio and the District of Columbia -- reporting it in their indices. The two Canadian Province indices report different numbers of pollutants; the smaller agency, Alberta, reports five air pollutants, while the larger, Ontario, reports only two.

2. Index Classification System

To facilitate comparisons of the various air pollution indices, an index classification system was developed.

TABLE 8

VARIABLES USED IN STATE-WIDE AND PROVINCE-WIDE
AIR POLLUTION INDICES

	Size	CO	SO_2	NO_2	Ox	COH	TSP
State							
District of Columbia	14	●	●	●	●	●	
Minnesota	37	●	●				●
New Jersey	170	●	●		●	●	
New York	237	●	●			●	
Ohio	228	●	●	●	●		●
Total		5	5	2	3	3	2
Province							
Alberta	26	●	●	●	●	●	
Ontario	70		●			●	

41

Although nearly every city with a daily index employs a different calculation method and different air quality categories, it was found that the various indices could be classified according to four criteria:

- Number of variables included in the index.

- Calculation method used to compute the index.

- Calculation mode (combined or uncombined).

- Descriptor categories reported with the index.

Categories which appear broad enough to group all the air pollution indices were developed from these criteria.

Number of Variables. This number designates the number of variables incorporated into an air pollution index. These variables include the five NAAQS pollutants (excluding hydrocarbons), visibility, and particle scattering.

Calculation Method. According to the index classification system, there are four calculation methods, three of which (Types A, B, and C) involve the use of an equation:

A. Nonlinear - Exponential function with coefficient or other nonlinear relationship. Coefficients may be constant or may vary, but relationship contains at least one variable raised to a power.

42

B. <u>Linear with nonconstant coefficients</u> - Segmented linear function of one or more variables or a product of variables. There are no exponents, but coefficients are different for different ranges of the variable C_1:

$$I = K_1 (C) C_1$$

C. <u>Linear with constant coefficients</u> - Linear function of one or more variables with coefficients that do not change:

$$I = K_1 C_1$$

Coefficients may be chosen as $K_1 = 1/C_{s_i}$, where C_{s_i} is standard for pollutant, giving a proportionate relationship; or they may be chosen as $K_1 = 100/C_{s_i}$ which gives percentage relationship; or they may be arbitrary and not related to any standard.

D. <u>Actual concentration values</u> - Concentrations reported in scientific units ($\mu g/m^3$, ppm) or standard units from some commonly used measurement technique (COH's, etc.).

An agency reporting just its actual concentration values is classified as not having an index and is not coded; however, when the agency reports actual concentrations and descriptor categories, its index is Type D.

The major nonlinear index (Type A) reviewed in this study is ORAQI.[12/] ORAQI is designed such that when each pollutant included in the index is equal to its standard, the index value is 100 (its critical value). In general, the values for ORAQI may be determined from the nomograph shown in Figure 3 or computed from the ORAQI equation. The nomograph is used by adding the pollutant concentrations on the "Summing Columns", placing this sum on the "Measured Total" column, and then drawing a line to the proper point on the "Unmeasured Pollutants" column. For example, when the sum is 20, and there are no unmeasured pollutants, the index is 28.

Alternatively, one may calculate ORAQI using the equation shown in Table 3. If less than five pollutants are used in the index, a different coefficient must be used. For example, for sulfur dioxide and particulate matter the equation is:

$$\text{ORAQI} = \left[14.42 \left(\frac{SO_2}{0.10} + \frac{PM}{150} \right) \right]^{1.37} \tag{1}$$

where

$\dfrac{SO_2}{0.10}$ = the 24-hour average concentration of sulfur dioxide (ppm) divided by a 0.10 ppm standard

$\dfrac{PM}{150}$ = the 24-hour average concentration of suspended particulate matter ($\mu g/m^3$) divided by a 150 $\mu g/m^3$ standard.

Figure 4 shows a plot of this equation for constant particulate matter (PM) concentrations (75, 150, and 225 $\mu g/m^3$).

44

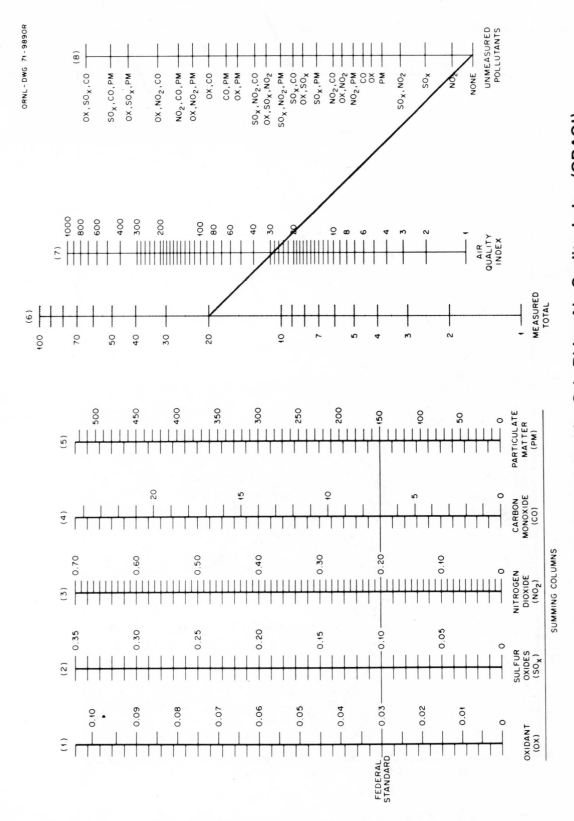

ORNL-DWG 71-9890R

Figure 3. Nomograph for determining the Oak Ridge Air Quality Index (ORAQI).

45

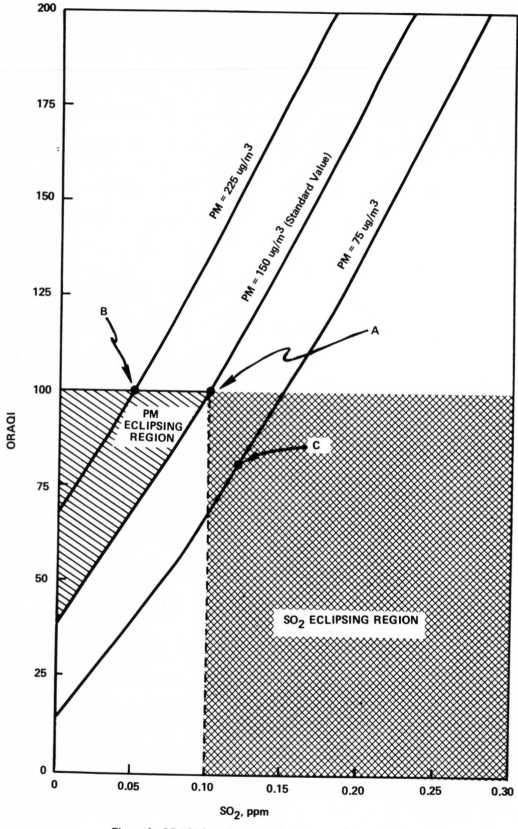

Figure 4. ORAQI function for sulfur dioxide and particulate matter.

The slight curvature (nonlinearity) of the lines is due to the exponent. When the two pollutants are exactly equal to the standards (0.10 ppm for SO_2, 150 $\mu g/m^3$ for PM), the index reaches its critical value of 100 (Point A). However, the index can be 100 under many other circumstances as well. For example, if the SO_2 concentration is 0.05 ppm. (below the standard), while the particulate concentration is 225 $\mu g/m^3$, the index is still I=100 (Point B), even through only one standard is exceeded.

A more important problem for this index is "eclipsing" -- the case when one pollutant exceeds its standard without the index exceeding its critical value. Suppose, for example, the SO_2 concentration is 0.12 ppm (above the SO_2 standard) and the particulate concentration is 75 $\mu g/m^3$ (Point C). Then the index value is I=80, and the SO_2 standard is exceeded but the index remains below its critical value. All possible index values for SO_2 eclipsing are shown in the "SO_2 Eclipsing Region" of Figure 4. A similar region can be identified for the case where particulate matter exceeds its standard and SO_2 is below its standard.

The Type B segmented linear calculation method (linear with nonconstant coefficients) is much simpler than the

Type A nonlinear method. Figure 5 shows a plot of the segmented linear function for carbon monoxide used in the Washington, D.C. index. Each pair of values (CO, I) are the coordinates of a breakpoint (represented as a dot). The resulting function consists of five straight line segments, each with different slope. The index value for any concentration of carbon monoxide can be determined directly from the curve. For example at 80 ppm CO, the index value is 200.

In the Type C (linear with constant coefficients) calculation method, the index value is a simple linear function of a pollutant concentration. The Type D method reports actual pollutant concentrations and therefore uses no index equation.

Calculation Mode. Another important aspect of the calculation method is how the index variables are treated. Does the agency report individual index values for each variable? Does the agency report an index value only for the variable which has the maximum value of all the index variables? Does the agency's index combine the variables in some fashion? Thus, the mode identifies whether the index is combined or uncombined. Uncombined indices include

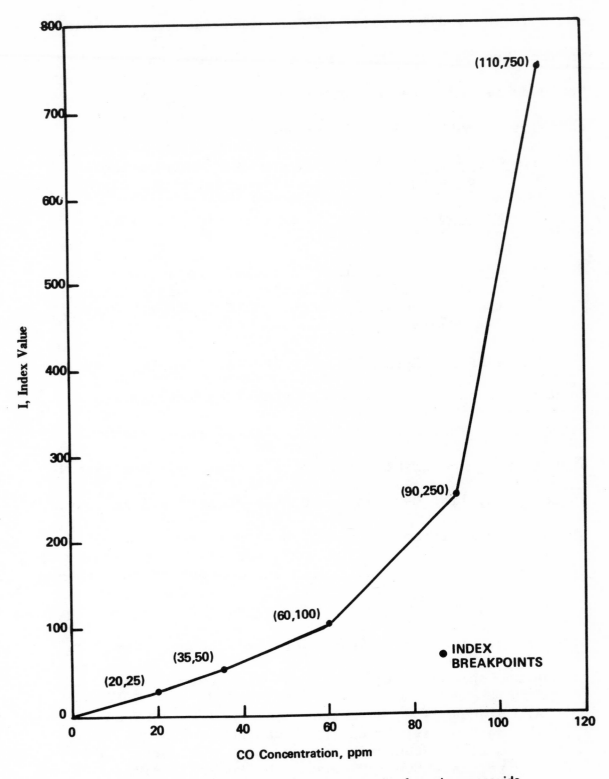

Figure 5. Example of a segmented linear function for carbon monoxide

those in the individual or maximum mode category; combined

indices are sometimes referred to as aggregated indices.

The mode is indicated by appending a subscript to the

calculation method classification.

1. <u>Individual</u> - An index value for each variable
   comprising the index is reported.

2. <u>Maximum</u> - Only the index value for the maximum
   variable is reported.

3. <u>Combined</u> - The index variables are aggregated,
   through some type of mathematical manipulation,
   to give one index value. (This mode exhibits
   the eclipsing effect.)

<u>Descriptor Categories</u>. The descriptor categories

result when the index range is subdivided into several

categories. The words assigned to these categories give

a qualitative description of the air quality. For example,

an index may list 0-25 as "good," 26-50 as "satisfactory,"

51-99 as "unsatisfactory," and 100-199 as "unhealthy."

If an index reports actual pollutant concentrations, then

several concentration ranges may be used for the descriptor

categories. Index descriptor categories can be based on

standards, episode criteria, or an arbitrary basis:

A. <u>Standards</u> - The category breakdown is based
   on Federal, State, or local ambient air
   quality standards -- for example, index
   values above 100 exceed the Federal Primary

NAAQS and those below fall into several categories partially based on the Federal Secondary NAAQS. If actual concentrations are reported, then these concentrations are related to the standards.

B. Episode Criteria - Type A (above) is extended to accommodate index values above 100. These values are based on the Federal, State, or local episode criteria -- for example, 100 is the Alert Stage, 200 is the Warning Stage, etc. For indices reporting actual pollutant concentrations, these concentrations are related to the episode criteria.

C. Arbitrary - Categories of this type are semiempirically based and usually designed to fit the specific requirements of the index values. This classification also covers indices with no descriptor categories.

Summary and Example Application of the Index

Classification System. The result of the classification system is a four-character code which describes any index. Using the system, the Oak Ridge Air Quality Index (ORAQI) is coded as "$5A_3A$" (Figure 6). The number "5" indicates that the index includes five pollutants or variables; "A_3" denotes the calculation method and mode (i.e., it is nonlinear and the variables are combined to give one index value); "A" refers to the basis for the descriptor categories (i.e., the categories reported with this index are based on the NAAQS).

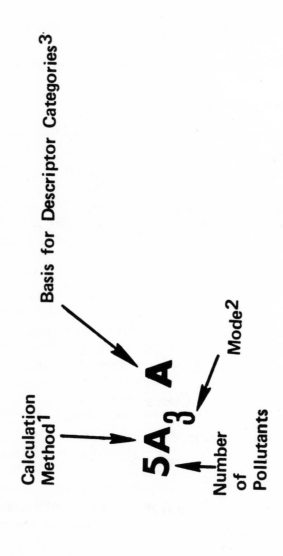

Calculation Method[1]

Basis for Descriptor Categories[3]

5A₃ A

Mode[2]

Number of Pollutants

[1] A: Nonlinear
B: Segmented linear
C: Linear
D: Actual Concentrations

[2] 1: Individual
2: Maximum
3: Combined

[3] A: Standards
B: Episode Criteria
C: Arbitary

Figure 6. Index Classification System

3. <u>Results of Classification</u>

The classification system described in the previous section was applied to all the indices reviewed in this study.

<u>Indices Reported in the Literature</u>. Table 9 shows the classification the eight indices reviewed in Chapter IV. Seven of the eight use a combined calculation mode (Type 3), and five of these use a nonlinear (Type A) calculation method. The general complexity of the "A_3" type index equation, with its inherent eclipsing effect, may have contributed to the limited use of these indices by local air pollution control agencies.

<u>Indices Reviewed in the Survey</u>. Application of the index classification system to the 30 index systems reviewed in the survey revealed 15 <u>basic</u> types[*] (Table 10). To simplify comparison of these index types, they are grouped according to their calculation method. Only Type B has no discontinued indices. The three discontinued indices apparently were dropped because they were not consistent with air pollution levels as preceived by the public.

---

[*]A basic type refers to the calculation method and descriptor categories, but not to the number of variables.

TABLE 9

CLASSIFICATION OF INDICES REPORTED IN THE LITERATURE

Index	Classification
Oak Ridge Air Quality Index (ORAQI)	nA_3A, $n=1$ to 5
Mitre Air Quality Index (MAQI)	nA_3A, $n=1$ to 5
Extreme Value Index (EVI)	nA_3A, $n=1$ to 4
Ontario Air Pollution Index (API)	$2A_3B$
Green's Combined Index (CI)	$2A_3C$
Combustion Products Index (CPI)	$1C_1C$
Air Quality Index (AQI)	nC_3C, $n=1$ to 5
PINDEX	$7C_3C$

TABLE 10

THE 15 INDEX TYPES AND THEIR USERS

Type	Users
A_1C	Detroit, Oklahoma City,[a] Memphis
A_3A	Tampa
A_3B	Minnesota, Ontario
A_3C	Alberta
B_2B	Baltimore, Ohio, Seattle, Washington, D.C.
B_2C	Denver
B_3C	Philadelphia
C_1C	Nashville
C_3B	Louisville, Pittsburgh, Dallas
C_3C	Jacksonville, Miami, Atlanta, Phoenix[a]
D_1A	New Jersey, New York State
D_1B	Anaheim, Los Angeles
D_1C	Connecticut,[a] Portland, Chattanooga
D_2A	New York City
D_2B	San Francisco

[a] Discontinued index

55

City/County Indices. Classification of the various indices used by the survey respondents revealed a striking diversity and few clear patterns (Table 11). A detailed analysis, however, reveals some important results.

Of the 33 city/county agencies, 13 (40 percent) include five variables in their index calculation (Table 12). This is due mainly to the fact that five agencies in Ohio and four in the Baltimore-Washington, D.C., area use indices incorporating five variables. In fact, each of these nine agencies used the $5B_2B$ type of index.

TABLE 12

NUMBER OF VARIABLES INCLUDED IN INDEX CALCULATION

Number of Variables	Number of Agencies	Percent
1	5	15
2	5	15
3	8	24
4	1	3
5	13	40
6	1	3
Total	33	100

TABLE 11

SUMMARY OF INDEX CLASSIFICATION RESULTS

	Number of Variables						Calculation Method				Mode			Descriptor Categories			
---	---	---	---	---	---	---	---	---	---	---	---	---	---	Type			Number
	1	2	3	4	5	6	A	B	C	D	1	2	3	A	B	C	
City/County																	
Anaheim, CA			●							●	●				●		3
Los Angeles, CA			●							●	●				●		3
San Francisco, CA				●						●		●				●	6
Denver, CO		●						●				●				●	5
Washington, DC					●			●				●			●		7
Jacksonville, FL						●			●				●			●	None
Miami, FL					●				●				●			●	5
Tampa, FL					●		●						●	●			6
Atlanta, GA			●						●				●			●	None
Louisville, KY					●				●				●		●		4
Baltimore, MD					●			●				●			●		8
Montgomery Co., MD					●			●				●			●		7
Detroit, MI	●						●				●				●	●	5
St. Paul, MN			●				●			●	●				●		4
Albany, NY			●							●	●			●			3
Buffalo, NY			●							●	●			●			3
Mineola, NY			●							●	●			●			3
New York City, NY					●					●	●			●			4
Rochester, NY			●							●	●			●			3
Akron, OH					●			●				●			●		12
Cincinnati, OH					●			●				●			●		12
Cleveland, OH					●			●				●			●		12
Dayton, OH					●			●				●			●		12
Toledo, OH					●			●				●			●		12
Portland, OR	●									●	●					●	5
Philadelphia, PA		●						●					●			●	3
Pittsburgh, PA		●							●				●			●	6
Chattanooga, TN	●									●	●					●	4
Memphis, TN	●						●				●					●	4
Nashville, TN	●								●		●					●	4
Dallas, TX		●							●			●			●		7
Fairfax Co., VA					●			●				●			●		3
Seattle, WA		●						●				●			●		3
State/Region																	
District of Columbia					●			●				●			●		7
Minnesota			●				●				●	●		●			4
New Jersey				●						●	●	●		●			3
New York		●								●	●				●		12
Ohio					●			●				●			●		12
Province																	
Alberta					●		●						●	●		●	5
Ontario		●					●						●		●		5

57

Despite the heavy influence of these nine agencies
on the data, Table 13 shows that the segmented linear
function (Type B) and the actual concentrations (Type D)
are the most popular calculation methods (37 and 30 percent, respectively). Only four cities (13 percent) use
a nonlinear index calculation, suggesting a definite
preference for the less complex calculation schemes.

TABLE 13

INDEX CALCULATION METHODS

Method	Number of Agencies[a]	Percent[a]
A. Nonlinear	4 (3)	12 (9)
B. Linear with nonconstant coefficients	12	37
C. Linear with constant coefficients	7	21
D. Actual concentration values	10 (11)	30 (33)
Total	33	100

[a] Numbers in parentheses are the reclassification of
agencies using two methods (see text).

This preference is also evident in St. Paul which uses a
nonlinear index (Type A: ORAQI), but in addition reports

actual concentration values (Type D). If St. Paul were reclassified as Type D (shown in parentheses, Table 13), then only three (9 percent) of the agencies use the nonlinear type calculation method.

Table 14 shows that the "maximum" mode of calculation was used by 13 (40 percent) of the agencies. Another 11 agencies (33 percent) used the "individual" mode, thus indicating a preference for uncombined (73 percent) versus combined (27 percent) indices. However, Jacksonville and St. Paul use both the individual and combined mode. If

TABLE 14

MODE OF INDEX CALCULATION

Mode	Number of Agencies[a]	Percent[a]
1. Individual	11 (13)	33 (40)
2. Maximum	13	40
3. Combined	9 (7)	27 (20)
Total	33	100

[a] Numbers in parentheses are the reclassification of agencies using two modes (see text).

59

they were reclassified as using the individual mode (as shown in parentheses, Table 14), then only seven (20 percent) of the agencies use the combined mode and 80 percent use the two uncombined modes.

Table 15 shows that 22 agencies (67 percent) used index descriptor categories based either on standards or on episode criteria; the remaining one-third used arbitrary categories.

TABLE 15

BASIS FOR INDEX DESCRIPTOR CATEGORIES

Category Basis	Number of Agencies	Percent
A. Standards	7	21
B. Episode criteria	15	46
C. Arbitrary	11	33
Total	33	100

The number of categories used in the indices is shown in the histogram of Figure 7. There appears to be a definite preference for three or four descriptor categories. However, there does not appear to be any tendency toward using the

60

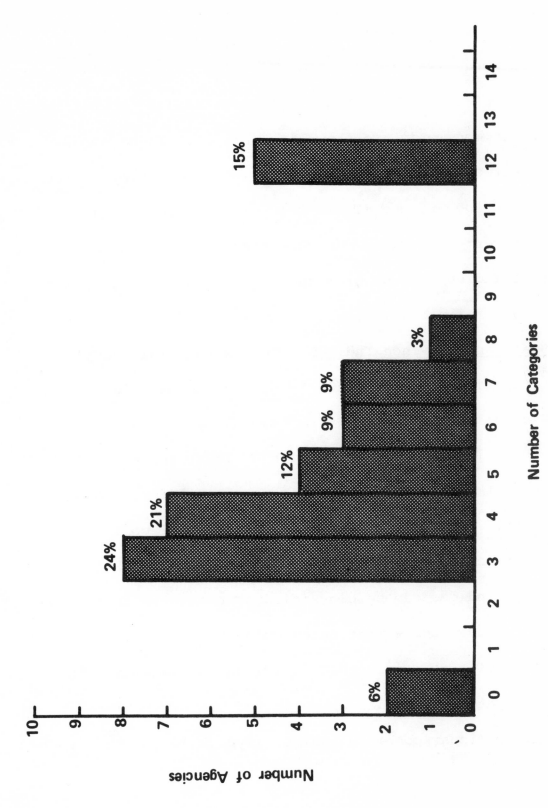

Figure 7. Histogram of the number of descriptor categories used in U.S. city and county air pollution indices.

same words for the descriptor categories. A total of 41
different words (Table 16) are used in the descriptor
categories of the 28 U.S. index systems. Indices containing
the more common words are shown in Table 17. These words
were selected by weighting each descriptor according to its
frequency of occurrence (Table 16). It is interesting to
note that certain words occur more frequently in multi-
pollutant indices and other words more frequently in indices
involving particulate matter.

State and Province Indices. Due to the small sample
size, only five States and two Provinces, no detailed
analysis was possible. However, examination of Table 11
shows that all of the States report at least three pollutants in their index; two States report all five NAAQS
pollutants. Since Minnesota reports individual pollutant
concentrations in addition to its combined index (ORAQI),
all States indices can be classified as using the segmented
linear or actual concentration calculation methods, while
the calculation mode is either individual or maximum. Thus,
both the States and cities make limited use of the more
complex, nonlinear combined indices (Type A_3). On the other

TABLE 16

THE FREQUENCY DISTRIBUTION OF THE 41 WORDS USED
FOR DESCRIPTOR CATEGORIES

Heavy	11	Normal	2
Good	10	Stage 1	2
Light	9	Stage 2	2
Unsatisfactory	7	Stage 3	2
Unhealthy(ful)	6	Very Heavy	2
Moderate	6	Warning	2
Emergency	5	Above Average	1
Poor	5	Acute	1
Extremely Heavy	4	Average	1
Fair	4	Below Average	1
Medium	4	Endangerment	1
Satisfactory	4	Extremely Poor	1
Severe	4	Harmful	1
Alert	3	High	1
Clean	3	Low	1
Extremely Light	3	Significant	1
Very Poor	3	Slight	1
Acceptable	2	Very Dangerous	1
Dangerous	2	Very Good	1
Excellent	2	Very Light	1
Hazardous	2		

TABLE 17

INDICES USING THE MORE COMMONLY OCCURRING WORDS
IN DESCRIPTOR CATEGORIES

Multipollutant Indices	Indices for Particulate Matter Only
<u>New York City</u> Good Acceptable Unsatisfactory Unhealthy <u>Minnesota, New Jersey</u> Good Satisfactory Unsatisfactory Unhealthful <u>Miami</u> Good Normal Moderate Heavy Severe	<u>Detroit, Memphis, (Oklahoma City)</u> Extremely light Light Medium Heavy Extremely heavy <u>Chattanooga</u> Light Moderate Heavy Alert

hand in Canada there appears to be a preference for this type of index, with both Alberta and Ontario using non-linear combined indices.

4.   Comments from Respondents

Some insight into the reasons for the great variety of air pollution indices was gained by examining the subjective views of the survey respondents. Their comments were assembled by the authors from notes taken during the informal telephone conversations with each agency (Appendix C). Since they do not represent official agency views, they are listed anonymously.

Agencies Using Indices. As one might expect, most individuals from agencies now using indices expressed satisfaction with their own index, although one respondent acknowledged that most people probably do not follow the index in the newspapers. There was widespread opinion that the numbers expressed by indices are not necessarily meaningful, and one agency stated that its index was not developed on any scientific basis and was not intended as such. In general, indices were viewed as an informational tool designed to advise the public as to the severity of air pollution levels, but not to convey any information about the deleterious effects of air pollution. Some agencies felt that the layman does not understand the technical language of air pollution, and thus indices fulfill an important need by communicating with him in a nontechnical way. However, in many cases the public may not understand the index either. One agency using the complex ORAQI index attempted to solve this problem by distributing a public information bulletin on the subject.

A number of the respondents expressed concern about the lack of spatial representativeness of index values. This concern apparently reflects a lack of representativeness of the monitoring data used to calculate the index.

Several agencies had found it necessary to make major changes in their indices within the past 5 years. These agencies indicated they had some difficulty overcoming the public confusion which resulted from these changes, particularly where the changes were great. One such agency stated that the introduction, right now, of any new indices "would bury us." Another agency changed its index from the combined form to a maximum type because the combined

66

index gave misleading results -- low values when one standard is violated and other pollutants are low, or high values when all pollutants are high but no standard is violated.

Agencies Not Using Indices. The diversity of opinion was wider among persons in agencies which do not presently use air pollution indices. Respondents often expressed dismay about the large number of air pollution indices in existence: With so many different air quality indices around, "people really can get confused when they move from city to city." Many respondents felt it better to familiarize the public with the scientific notation for pollutant concentrations -- $\mu g/m^3$, ppm -- than to teach the public how to understand an index. Some agencies felt they would adopt an index if they could find one that was understandable and agreeable to all, but that there is not yet a sufficient scientific basis for such an index. Some of the reasons offered for not adopting an air pollution index were purely practical -- not enough monitoring data to implement the index or not enough staff to compute the index. The problem of finding an index that is consistent

with the public's perception of air quality was cited
frequently as a reason for not using an index. One agency
used ORAQI for several years but found it did not correlate
well.with observed air quality and resulted in many complaints;
thus, it was abandoned:

> We soon found that [index values] did not relate
> to what the public saw. Many times, mountains
> surrounding [the city] would be barely visible
> during winter months and yet the index would
> register in the light air pollution range. This
> resulted in considerable controversy concerning
> the validity of the index with the general public
> and the news media. We went to considerable
> length to explain that the index was a combination
> of a number of pollutant levels and that the
> gaseous pollutants could be low and there could
> still be sufficient fine suspended particulates
> in the air to obscure visibility, resulting in
> a low combined index. After one year of increasing
> problems with the combined index which included
> several attempts to modify it, we discontinued its
> use.

Another agency suggested that the decision of whether or
not to use an index probably depends on the level of public
education, and that any approach is satisfactory as long
as the public fully understands it. Another agency felt
that it was preferable to forecast tomorrow's pollutant
values (or index values) than to announce today's or
yesterday's values, as many indices are designed to do.

A common reason given for not using an index had to do with the lack of clear understanding of indices by the public, leading to confusion and misunderstanding. One agency noted that most of the current indices, because they are arbitrary, are really not interpretable. As such, this respondent felt that most indices represent a "non-understandable, nondimensional number." One agency discontinued its index because the news media "sensationalized" it by reading more into the index than was intended: "The index is now at 80 and when it gets to 100 you will have to start worrying."

Criteria for a Uniform Index. Although some respondents expressed much skepticism about the understandability and meaningfulness of air pollution indices in general, particularly about combined air pollution indices, there was general agreement that prevailing confusion might be reduced if the Federal Government were to develop, endorse, and support a single, uniform air pollution index. Only two dissenting arguments were offered against this concept: One respondent felt that adoption of a uniform index would make comparisons of air pollution levels in different cities too easy, creating hostility among the cities.

Another respondent felt that each index should be tailored
to the public it serves and therefore should be different
in different cities. From the comments, it appears that
one of the most serious obstacles to adopting any standardized index is the fact that most cities already have one
and would have difficulty changing it to conform to some
uniform system. The process of re-educating the public
poses a difficult problem which would need to be addressed.
Another serious problem lies in formulating an index that
is truly satisfactory to these agencies and to their public.
From the viewpoints expressed by respondents, it appears
that any uniform air pollution index would have to possess
the following desirable features:

- Is easily understood by the public

- Is not inconsistent with perceived air
  pollution levels

- Is spatially meaningful

- Includes major air pollutants (and
  expandable to include future pollutants)

- Is calculated in a simple manner using
  reasonable assumptions

- Rests upon a solid scientific basis

- Relates to ambient air quality standards
  and goals

- Relates to episode criteria

- Exhibits day-to-day variation

- Can be forecast a day in advance
  (optional)

5. Display and Dissemination Techniques

The methods most frequently used to report air pollution indices to the public include the usual communications media: newspapers, television, radio, and telephone recordings. Of these, newspapers are the most common dissemination method, and they give air pollution indices the greatest coverage. Appendix D gives several examples of newspaper index reports; other examples can be found in recent reports by Cullen[20] and Reidy.[21] Some newspapers give only a narrative description, while others include a bar graph or table with a brief explanatory note of each day's index.

The next most prevalent means of reporting daily indices appears to be television. Television reports may give only the index value or include visual displays accompanied by a short verbal explanation. Of course, radio is limited to verbal reports. Index reporting formats vary not only from city to city but also within each city.

Thus, two newspapers in the same city (for example, Albany, New York -- see Appendix D) may use an entirely different format to report the same index; alternatively, one news-paper may not report the index at all. The same variation occurs in television and radio reports.

The diversity in reporting of indices apparently results largely from lack of involvement by the air pollution control agency in deciding how its index is to be reported to the public. Several agencies interviewed in this survey specif-ically stated that they do not recommend a format for reporting their index to the public. However, a few agencies indicated that they suggest display formats and recommend their use. In those agencies recommending no particular format, the resulting flexibility may lead not only to variations in who reports the index, but in how it is reported. If carried too far, this could have undesirable effects: in one city, for example, a television reporter "sensationalized" the index, causing the agency to discontinue its use altogether (see Section 4 of this chapter).

The use of telephone recordings (codophones) to disseminate air quality information generally is undertaken only by air pollution control agencies, although some citizens' groups operate telephone air pollution information services for persons with respiratory diseases. Those agencies using telephone recordings do so for the convenience of the news media and the public. The information on these recordings is updated regularly and, in contrast to newspapers and television, telephone recordings use a specific format, similar to that used by the telephone companies for the weather report.

In summary, there is much diversity in the way the various media report indices. It is not clear that these diverse approaches have solved the difficult problem of clearly relating an air pollution index to air pollution levels and making the result understandable to the layman. This situation possibly could be improved if the media used a standard reporting and display format. Such a format could be structured to facilitate public education about the origins of air pollution, its effects, and methods of control.

CHAPTER VII

A CASE STUDY OF THE DEVELOPMENT
OF A COMMON AIR QUALITY INDEX
FOR A TRI-STATE AREA

The region comprising the cities of Steubenville, Ohio;
Pittsburgh, Pennsylvania; and Wheeling, West Virginia, has
pioneered in establishing cooperative efforts to abate air
pollution. In 1970, the three States were the first to
establish an interstate compact to control air pollution.[22]
The compact was designed to curb emissions along the Ohio
River where there are major chemical, steel, aluminum, and
metallurgical plants, as well as electric power generating
stations.

At present, three different air pollution indices are
used in the region. During late 1974, representatives from
the Ohio Environmental Protection Agency, North Ohio Valley
Air Authority, Allegheny County Bureau of Air Pollution
Control (Pittsburgh), West Virginia Air Pollution Control
Commission, and Wheeling Air Pollution Control Board met
to discuss their indices, identify the problems associated
with developing a common index, and recommend criteria for
a common index.

The main reason for developing a common index within this tri-State region is to alleviate confusion resulting from public exposure to the three different indices. A common index could present a clear and unified reporting system of the air quality in the region.

These three indices are analyzed in detail in Appendix B. Briefly, Ohio's index reports the maximum of five subindex values which are calculated using segmented linear functions with nonconstant coefficients (Type $5B_2B$). The subindex for each variable is a percentage of the Ohio ambient air quality standard. The 12 descriptor categories of the index are based on the Ohio standards and alert criteria, in which a value of 100 indicates that the pollutant concentration has reached the Ohio ambient air quality standard.

The index used in Pittsburgh and surrounding Allegheny County combines SO_2 and COH in a linear fashion with constant coefficients (Type $2C_3B$). The index is the sum of the ratios of the pollutant concentrations to their standards, multiplied by 50. There are six descriptor categories based on the Allegheny County episode criteria. Due to the way in

which the two subindices are combined, a range of values
$(84 \leq I \leq 111)$ signifies onset of the first stage alert.

West Virginia, which is presently considering adoption
of a State-wide index, is awaiting the outcome of the
present discussions regarding development of a common
tri-State index. As an interim measure, the city of
Wheeling recently instituted ORAQI. This index uses
nonlinear exponential function with a constant coefficient
to calculate index values from the sum of the concentration/
standard ratios (Type nA_3A, with n= 1, 2, 3, 4, or 5). The
exponent, 1.37, and the coefficient, 5.7, are chosen to
give index values which relate to the secondary NAAQS. The
index also may be calculated using a nomograph. ORAQI has
six descriptor categories, and an index value of 100 is
intended to mean that all pollutant concentrations in the
index have reached the secondary standards. However, due
to the combined nature of the index, values of 100 may be
obtained under many different conditions.

The problems in developing a common index from three
indices which incorporate different numbers of pollutants,
calculation schemes, and descriptor categories are immense,

but not necessarily insurmountable. The three agencies
were acutely aware of the complexity of the task and the
extensive cooperation that would be required to meet the
goal.

One of the authors attended the second meeting of
officials from the three agencies. This meeting explored
the overall problems involved in developing a common index.
Each agency was asked to discuss its index and to provide
thoughts on developing possible criteria for a common index.
The following summarizes the most important points presented
by each agency.

West Virginia

- An index value of 100 should identify a
  significant point in the descriptor
  category scheme (e.g., violation of the
  short-term primary NAAQS or one of the
  Federal Episode Criteria).

- Indices containing too many subindices
  (i.e., combined indices) confuse the
  public and underemphasize the contribution
  of the subindex with the highest concentration.

- Because the present NAAQS do not consider synergism, a synergism term may not be appropriate in the index. However, synergistic SO_2-COH and SO_2-TSP terms are a part of the Federally recommended episode criteria.

- Using two indices, one for stationary source pollutants and one for mobile source pollutants, would inform the public of the two major categories of air pollution sources covered by different enforcement policies.

- The index would provide useful information about the effect of enforcement activities in the tri-State region.

- The index should be sensitive to the daily changes in air quality.

- In addition to issuing a common index, it may be useful to also issue a running annual average of the index, as well as

the number of days the standards have
been exceeded.

- Adoption of a common index will require
  the States to establish similar episode
  criteria.

Ohio

- Any index must maintain its credibility
  with the public; that is, it must reflect
  what is perceived and give a true
  representation of regional air quality.

- The index calculation should take all pollutants into consideration and be able to
  incorporate new pollutants. However, the
  index (1) should not include combined
  (synergistic) terms for which standards do
  not exist, and (2) should not be structured
  to allow identification of individual sources.

- The problem of obtaining spatially representative index values may be partly solved
  by reporting mean or maximum values over
  the region.

79

Allegheny County

- The numerical range of descriptor categories
  for the index must take into account the
  fact that future air quality levels (and
  hence index values) will be lower than
  those presently experienced.

- The primary and secondary NAAQS and the
  recommended Federal Episode Criteria
  should be used in defining the descriptor
  categories.

- Separate indices for mobile sources and
  stationary sources have the advantage that
  they educate the public about pollutant-
  source relationships. A separate index
  for each pollutant would not be as ef-
  fective an educational tool.

- The SO_2-COH index now used in Allegheny
  County is adequate for most of the year,
  but it could be supplemented in the summer
  months by an index emphasizing the presence
  of oxidant.

In the general discussion that followed, several concrete recommendations were made:

- The three jurisdictions should develop a common system for the descriptor categories accompanying the index. (It was noted that each jurisdiction would have some problems in adapting its present system to any new system. Such a change should be permanent -- not to be changed in the near future by Federal regulations.)

- The index should be calculated in relationship to air quality standards, with possibly a second index for the running annual average value of the index.

- Public information (daily index reports) and official air pollution control activities should not be reported together.

- Further efforts to develop a common index should also include the States of Pennsylvania, Kentucky, and Maryland.

At the end of the meeting tentative agreement was reached on the following point:

- The value of 100 on the tri-State air
  quality index scale should indicate
  that the short-term primary NAAQS for
  at least one air pollutant has been
  violated.

In summary, this second meeting enabled the three
agencies to learn which modifications will have to be made
in existing indices if a common index is adopted. In
addition, the discussion of the general criteria for such
an index laid the preliminary ground work for development
of a uniform index to serve the three States.

The third meeting of the tri-State agency officials
took place in Columbus, Ohio, on January 30, 1975. The
meeting was a general review of the previous meeting with
some additional discussion on the following points:

- The three main areas of agreement required
  to establish a common index are the selection
  of a numerical scale, the definition of
  category divisions and descriptors, and
  the determination of how the index should
  relate to the episode criteria presently
  used by Ohio and Pittsburgh.

- Each State reviewed the official decision-making process it must go through before changing its current index.

- Each agency expressed the hope that a common index system could be operational by the end of summer 1975.

As of July 1, 1975 no final decisions had been made on adopting a common tri-State index.

CHAPTER VIII

CONCLUSIONS

Air pollution indices perform a service by giving residents of urban areas an indication of day-to-day changes in air quality. However, air quality levels observed in urban areas also are of interest to the Nation as a whole because they provide an indication of the Nation's progress toward cleaner air and can allow comparisons of the air pollution problems in different cities. Such information is of particular importance to national decision makers.

It would be helpful if the daily air pollution indices in common use facilitated interpretation of national air quality. Unfortunately, they appear to impede it, and their diversity appears to confuse the issue. With so many different indices in use in metropolitan areas, it becomes impossible, on a national level, to gain insight into metropolitan air pollution levels by examining the indices. Further, with little assurance that the data on which each index is based are of the same quality and manipulated in the same fashion, it becomes difficult to interpret the meaning of each index and virtually impossible to use the index to compare metropolitan air pollution problems or to assess air quality trends over time. While a given index might be suitable for application on a metropolitan scale, all the indices, when taken together, give a picture of confusion.

The need is clear for a uniform air pollution index which can be used nationwide. From the comments of air pollution control agency personnel, there is evidence that a standardized air pollution index system, or a uniform air quality reporting format, would be both beneficial and welcome. In a recent report,[2/] the National Academy of Sciences recommended that a "uniform national system of air quality indices be developed and adopted." However, one major question remains unanswered: What should be the structure of the uniform index?

As a first step toward refining this structure, this study has identified criteria for a uniform air pollution index (Chapter VI, Section 4). Using these criteria, along with the survey data and major findings, it has been possible to develop two prototype air pollution indices -- the Standardized Urban Air Quality Index (SUAQI), and the Primary Standards Index which are discussed in Appendices E and F. They are offered to provide examples of the characteristics that such an index should possess, and should be viewed only as a starting point from which to develop an acceptable nationwide index.

The great variation in existing indices suggests there may be great variation in monitoring practices as well. If a standardized urban air pollution index were adopted, the index would not be comparable from city to city unless the data on which it is based were of the same high quality. Thus, quality assurance (proper measurement methods, instrument configuration, laboratory practices) is critical if the index is to have uniform meaning and applicability. One approach to help insure that the data used in the index are of adequate quality is to provide standard procedures for the way in which the agency collects the data for the index. Ultimately, each city might have its own standardized "index reference site," which conforms to these procedures. A first step in this process is for the Federal Government to publish an Index Monitoring Guidelines document, which would specify such factors as: (1) pollutants used in the index, (2) method of calculation, (3) descriptor categories, (4) averaging time for the pollutants, (5) period of the day in which averaging times should begin, (6) measurement methods to be used for each pollutant, (7) monitoring system configuration (for example, inlet diameter and flow rates), (8) height of sampling probe, and (9) procedures for selecting monitoring station sites.

Decisions as to the nature and structure of any uniform index are complex and should rest on informed judgment. The data base developed in this study should provide much of the information required to arrive at these decisions. Since the selection of a uniform index is largely a policy matter, it is recommended that a Federal interagency committee be formed to review this study, along with the relevant data, and to arrive at conclusions as to the feasibility of establishing a national air quality index or data reporting format. This interagency committee also should oversee the development of the Index Monitoring Guidelines document, which would be used to familiarize State and local air pollution agencies with the nature and characteristics of the standardized air pollution index.

CHAPTER IX

FUTURE RESEARCH NEEDS

Although this investigation has provided much information that will be of assistance in establishing a uniform index or data reporting format, this study is by no means the final step in such a process. Further research should be undertaken to improve knowledge on important related topics:

- Scientific Basis

- Public Attitudes

- Index Reporting Systems

- Monitoring Siting

- Follow-up Study

1. Scientific Basis

One possible explanation for the great diversity of air pollution indices in current use is the lack of a uniform scientific basis. Knowledge of the relationship between observed effects and air pollutant concentrations over a wide concentration range is very limited. The problem of generating a meaningful dose-response relationship from studies of health effects, for example, is extremely formidable. Possibly, future research on the health effects of air pollution may enable dose-response functions to be established on which a more scientifically defensible index could be proposed. Lacking such functions, some agencies choose a linear calculation method, some a segmented linear method, and some a nonlinear method. Because there is no solid basis for any one approach, indices become arbitrary in design and subject purely to the judgment of the air pollution agency involved. Progress toward solving this problem could be achieved by additional scientific research on the effects of air pollutants on humans, on plants and animals, and on materials.

2. Public Attitudes

In the authors' experience, there appears to be much controversy among members of the professional air pollution community as to the meaning and significance of air pollution indices. Some of this controversy results from varied assumptions about the public's attitudes toward indices. Some air pollution professionals believe that indices are interpreted by the public to mean that the air is "healthy" or "unhealthy" and that members of the public actually may modify their behavior due to index reports (that is, they may stay indoors, take trips, or reduce their physical activity).

Other air pollution professionals feel that indices are interpreted by the public as a relative measure of the clarity of the air (for example, as a day to day measure of visibility) with little other significance.

Among the agencies, some felt that members of the community paid considerable attention to the index, were pleased with it, and used it in their daily activity; other agencies felt that their index confused the public but was nevertheless necessary because the community wanted a simple indicator of air pollution; still other agencies felt that the public probably didn't even know the index existed.

This lack of agreement about the community's feelings toward indices suggests there is need to obtain more knowledge about the public's perception and attitudes toward indices than has been possible in the present study. Do high index values, for example, actually cause changes in behavior on the part of individuals? Such behavior changes could, in turn, affect daily fuel consumption (increased use of indoor lighting and appliances; increased use of energy for travel) and have other social costs. In those communities where high index values occur frequently, residents may be more inclined to purchase electrostatic

precipitators, to limit their outdoor physical activity,

or to advise other potential residents not to move there.

They may even consider moving elsewhere -- to a city where

air pollution is less a "problem."[*] The limited information

available about the public's perception of air pollution

indices suggests that future research to examine, in-depth,

the public's views toward indices and the use they make of

these indices would be helpful. The data of the present

study should provide a sound basis for selecting the cities

in which such an attitude study could be carried out. Such

a study might possibly include three or more communities,

each having very different indices, with opinion interviews

of a random sample of respondents. It might examine the

ways in which they understand environmental problems in

general, their level of exposure to the media, and the manner

in which indices are interpreted and are useful to them.

---

[*]During this study, one of the authors was contacted
by a person who was considering job offers in two different
Southern California cities. He wanted to know the frequency
at which the air pollution index in each city reached unhealthy values. Since the two cities used different indices,
no comparison was possible, and no information could be
given to assist him in making the decision.

3.   Index Reporting Systems

The air pollution index can provide a mechanism for
reporting air quality data to the public. Most of the
agencies which do not use indices, as defined here,
nevertheless report their actual pollutant concentrations
in daily newspapers, or in weekly or monthly agency
publications. Although extensive information on this subject
is not available, the materials provided by the agencies
indicate there is great variety in the ways in which air
quality data are reported and the media used. Some agencies
list the concentrations of all pollutants; some list just
several. Some list the air quality standards alongside the
data; some do not. It is probable that a uniform reporting
format could be established for reporting air quality data,
as one recent paper has suggested.[23] Before this is done,
it would be useful to survey in greater detail the ways in
which agencies now report their air quality data to the public.
A research project focusing on different air quality reporting
formats, with emphasis on the public's acceptance and com-
prehension of these formats, would be most useful for this
purpose.

4. Monitoring Siting

One of the most common air monitoring problems --
the selection of suitable air monitoring sities -- also
surfaces when air pollution indices are considered.
Several respondents in this survey strongly emphasized
this problem. When data are generated at several air
monitoring locations in an urban area, which location or
locations should be used for computing the index? Because
of the complexity of this problem, and the variations in
air monitoring networks, insufficient data was obtained to
provide insight into the ways in which agencies currently
solve this problem.

However, there was some evidence that many air pollution
agencies, faced with the problem of deciding which air
monitoring site to use in computing their index, selected the
station having the "maximum" concentrations. Others,
arbitrarily chose a "downtown" location, irrespective of its
concentration levels; still others obtained an average of
several locations. Because of the importance of this problem,
and the complex issues it raises, it is recommended that an
extensive survey be conducted of site locations, the basis
for choosing different sites, and the way in which choice of
site affects index values.

5. Follow-up Study

The approach used to gather much of the information in this study -- solicitation of information by telephone -- proved itself to be a powerful means for inexpensively gathering large quantities of data on a national scale. The data permit drawing a comprehensive picture of national practices regarding air pollution indices, but the present study does not probe deeply into monitoring and data reporting practices in each metropolitan area. For a more in-depth analysis of these factors, written questionnaires could be used, or on-site interviews conducted with air pollution control agency personnel. It is recommended, in future follow-up studies, that these more intensive survey methods be considered.

If a standardized air pollution index were proposed by the Federal Government, it would be desirable to survey attitudes of the technical staffs of U.S. air pollution agencies toward this new index. Such a follow-up survey could provide valuable insights into whether the index is formulated properly; it would also give an indication of the liklihood that air pollution control agencies will

successfully adopt the index. The follow-up survey could
be accomplished through a carefully designed, written
questionnaire accompanied by a description of the index.
The written questionnaire could be followed by personal
interviews at selected air pollution agencies, particularly
those agencies expressing unclear or ambiguous feelings
about the index. The goal of the follow-up survey should
be to determine any unsatisfactory characteristics of the
proposed index, changes necessary to correct these problems,
and obstacles which may impede adoption of a standardized
index. The follow-up survey also should examine the
response of air pollution control agency personnel toward
any standardized monitoring procedures designed to improve
the quality of data for the index.

REFERENCES

1. "Environmental Quality-1973 -- The Fourth Annual Report of the Council on Environmental Quality," Washington, D.C., 1973.

2. "Planning for Environmental Indices," Report of the Planning Committee on Environmental Indices to the Environmental Studies Board, National Research Council, National Academy of Sciences, Preliminary Final Report, September 30, 1974.

3. ."The National Environmental Indices: Air Quality and Outdoor Recreation," MTR-6159, The Mitre Corporation, McLean, Va., 1972.

4. "Environmental Quality-1972 -- The Third Annual Report of the Council on Environmental Quality," Washington, D.C., August 1972.

5. Public Law 88-206, as amended by Public Law 91-604, 84 Stat. 1676 (42 U.S.C. 1857 et. seq.).

6. "National Primary and Secondary Ambient Air Quality Standards," Federal Register, Vol. 36, No. 84, April 30, 1971, pp. 8186-8201.

7. "Requirements for Preparation, Adoption, and Submittal of Implementation Plans," Federal Register, Vol. 36, No. 158, August 14, 1971, pp. 15486-15506.

8. Green, M.H., "An Air Pollution Index Based on Sulfur Dioxide and Smoke Shade," J. Air Poll. Control Assoc., 11, 703 (1966).

9. Shenfeld, L., "Note on Ontario's Air Pollution Index and Alert System," J. Air Poll. Control Assoc., 20, 612 (1970).

10. McAdie, H.G., and D.K.A. Gillies," The Operational Forecasting of Undesirable Pollution Levels Based on a Combined Pollution Index," J. Air Poll. Control Assoc., 23, 941 (1973).

11. Babcock, L.R., "A Combined Pollution Index for Measurement of Total Air Pollution," _J. Air Poll. Control Assoc._, _20_, 653 (1970).

12. Thomas, W.A., L.R. Babcock, Jr., and W.D. Shults, "Oak Ridge Air Quality Index," ORNL-NSF-EP-8, Oak Ridge National Laboratory, Oak Ridge, Tenn., September 1971.

13. Miller, T.L., "Short Time Averaging Relationships to Air Quality Standards (STARAQS) -- A Predictive Air Quality Index Model for Use by Air Pollution Control Agencies," Paper #73-351, Presented at the 66th Annual Meeting of the Air Pollution Control Association, June 1973.

14. Rich, T.A., "Air Pollution Studies Aided by Overall Air Pollution Index," _Env. Sci. and Tech._, _1_, 796 (1967).

15. Fensterstock, J.C., K. Goodman, G.M. Duggan, and W.S. Baker, "The Development and Utilization of an Air Quality Index," Paper #69-73, Presented at the 62nd Annual Meeting of the Air Pollution Control Association, June 1969.

16. Bisselle, C.A., "Strategic Environmental Assessment System: Air and Water Pollution Indicators," MTR-6565, The Mitre Corporation, McLean, Va., April 1974.

17. "National Environmental Policy Act of 1969 -- Environmental Indices -- Status of Development Pursuant to Sections 102(2)(B) and 204 of the Act," Committee on Interior and Insular Affairs, United States Senate, December 1973.

18. "Indicators of Environmental Quality," W.A. Thomas, Ed., Plenum, New York, N.Y., 1972.

19. "1973-1974 Directory of Governmental Air Pollution Agencies," Air Pollution Control Association, Pittsburgh, Pa., 1973.

20. Cullen, J.J., T.V. Flaherty, Jr., and S.M. Barnett, "Indices for Dissemination of Ambient Air Quality Information to the Public," Paper #74-221, Presented at the 67th Annual Meeting of the Air Pollution Control Association, June 1974.

21. Reidy, M., and C. Dziewulski, "Homogeneous Dissemination of Ambient Air Quality Levels to the News Media and the Public or the Need to Eschew Obfuscation," Paper #73-352, Presented at the 66th Annual Meeting of the Air Pollution Control Association, June 1973.

22. "Ohio-West Virginia Air Compact Is Approved," Env. Sci. and Tech., 4, 182 (1970).

23. Hunt, W.F., W.M. Cox, W.R. Ott, and G. Thom, "A Common Air Quality Reporting Format: Precursor to an Air Quality Index," Presented at the Fifth Annual Environmental Engineering and Science Conference, Louisville, Ky., March 1975.

APPENDIX A

<u>AIR POLLUTION INDEX DATA SHEET</u>

I.   Agency

       Agency Name: _____

       Address: _____

                   _____

                   _____

       Telephone Number: _____

       Number of Staff (Total):   _____

II.   Does the Agency use an Air Pollution Index?

               Yes _____   No _____

       <u>If yes</u>, what is it called?   _____

          Length of years in use: _____

          Purpose of Index: _____

       <u>If no</u>, why?   _____

       _____

III. <u>If yes</u>, what parameters are covered in the Index?

      _____

      _____

        a.   Equation for calculating Index: _____

        b.   Method of converting averaging times to Index values (i.e., factors):   _____

            _____

        c.   Range of values for Index: _____

            _____

d. Method of interpreting, e.g., air quality categories, Index for stated uses:

_____

_____

e. Frequency which Index is reported and time period to which it applies:

_____

f. Number and selection the monitoring sites which provide data for Index:

_____

g. Can any literature or write-up on the index be provided? Yes ___ No ___

h. What are the advantages and disadvantages of using this Index?

_____

_____

IV. Additional Comments: _____

_____

_____

_____

_____

INDEX ANALYSIS RECORD

LOCATION

Phoenix, Arizona

PHONE

(602) 258-6381

AGENCY

Maricopa County Health Department
Environmental Services Division
Bureau of Air Pollution Control
1825 East Roosevelt
Phoenix, Arizona 85006

AGENCY SIZE

25

VARIABLES

[X] CO [X] NO_2 [ ] PARTICULATE [ ] PART. SCATTER

[ ] SO_2 [X] O_3 [X] COH [ ] VISIBILITY

[ ] STATE

[X] CITY/county

CLASSIFICATION

$4C_3C$

CATEGORIES

0- 25	Clean Air
26- 50	Light Air Pollution
51- 75	Moderate Air Pollution
76-100	Heavy Air Pollution
>100	Severe Air Pollution

RANGE

0-100+

EQUATION

$$I = 2(O_x) + (NO_2) + (CO) + 10(COH)$$

DESCRIPTION

The index was based on the "Combined Air Pollution Index" previously developed by the San Francisco Bay Area Air Pollution Control District (BAAPCD). It was computed from monitoring data at the control station at 1845 East Roosevelt Street, Phoenix. The index was found to be inconsistent with the public's "perceived" impression of air pollution levels. That is, the mountains surrounding Phoenix would often be barely visible during the winter months and yet the index would register in the light air pollution range. This inconsistency produced much controversy by the public and news media regarding the validity of the index. After one year of increasing problems with this combined index, it was discontinued. (The early BAAPCD index, on which this index was modeled, also was discontinued in San Francisco for essentially the same reasons.)

A number of other air pollution indices also were evaluated using the Phoenix air monitoring data (ORAQI, M.U.R.C., etc.). In all cases, problems were encountered due to inconstencies of each index with perceived visibility reduction.

MONITORING INFORMATION

2 full continuous air monitoring stations with 7 additional stations measuring CO, and in most cases, O_3, COH, TSP; all 9 stations are attached to a minicomputer.

REPORTING FREQUENCY

11 A.M. Daily

LENGTH OF TIME IN USE

Initiated 7/1/70
Discontinued in 1971

INDEX ANALYSIS RECORD

LOCATION	AGENCY
Anaheim, California	Orange County Air Pollution Control District
	811 N. Broadway Street
PHONE	Santa Ana, California 92701
(714)834-5370	

AGENCY SIZE	VARIABLES				CLASSIFICATION
24	[X] CO	[ ] NO$_2$	[ ] PARTICULATE	[ ] PART. SCATTER	3D$_1$B
[ ] STATE [X] CITY/county	[X] SO$_2$	[X] O$_3$	[ ] COH	[ ] VISIBILITY	

CATEGORIES

EPISODE CRITERIA:

CO, ppm		SO$_2$, ppm		Oxidant, ppm	
(1-hr.)	(12-hr.)	(1-hr.)	(24-hr.)	(1-hr.)	
40	20	0.5	0.2	0.2	Stage 1
75	35	1.0	0.7	0.4	Stage 2
100*	50	2.0	0.9	0.6*	Stage 3

*Concentration to last for one-hour and predicted to persist for one additional hour

RANGE: Actual Concentrations

EQUATION: N/A

DESCRIPTION

   The previous system in use for approximately 2 years was based on the Smog Alert system previously operated in Los Angeles for 20 years. The old Los Angeles system was based on instantaneous concentration maxima. It was intended to advise school children and other sensitive persons to curtail strenuous activities with the onset of moderately high air pollution levels (See Los Angeles Index Analysis Record). The new episode system was initiated in April 1974 to comply with requirements of the California State Air Resources Board. It is identical to the Los Angeles episode system, except that the Los Angeles system also includes instantaneous maxima in its episode criteria.

MONITORING INFORMATION	REPORTING FREQUENCY	LENGTH OF TIME IN USE
8 continuous air monitoring stations covering 6 different source-receptor zones	Reported only when stated levels are exceeded.	Adopted April 10, 1974. Replaces previous system in use for 2 years

INDEX ANALYSIS RECORD

LOCATION

Los Angeles, California

PHONE

(213)974-7411

AGENCY

Los Angeles County Air Pollution Control District
434 S. San Pedro Street
Los Angeles, California 90013

CLASSIFICATION

$3D_1B$

AGENCY SIZE

380

VARIABLES

[X] CO   [ ] NO_2 [ ] PARTICULATE   [ ] PART. SCATTER

[X] SO_2 [X] O_3 [ ] COH   [ ] VISIBILITY

[ ] STATE

[X] CITY

CATEGORIES

EPISODE CRITERIA:

CO, ppm		SO_2, ppm		Oxidant, ppm	
(1-hr.)	(12-hr.)	(1-hr.)	(24-hr.)	(1-hr.)	
40	20	0.5	0.2	0.2	Stage 1
75	35	1.0	0.7	0.4	Stage 2
100*	50	2.0	0.9	0.6*	Stage 3

*Concentration to last for one-hour and predicted to persist for one additional hour

RANGE

Actual Concentrations

EQUATION

N/A

DESCRIPTION

The episode criteria also include the following instantaneous maxima:

	CO, ppm	NO_x, ppm	SO_2, ppm	O_3, ppm
Stage 1:	50	3	3	.50
Stage 2:	100	5	5	1.0
Stage 3:	150	10	10	1.5

Previously, the Agency operated a "Smog Alert" system for 20 years which incorporated the above instantaneous maxima. The Agency also operated a "School and Health Smog Warning System" since July 2, 1969, which was intended to give protection from moderate air pollution levels to school students and persons with respiratory or cardiac disorders. Under this system, a "School Smog Warning" was issued for the air monitoring zone affected whenever the ozone forecast level exceeds 0.35 ppm (instantaneous) in any zone. The warning was issued to the mass media as part of the daily air pollution forecast for broadcast to the public and for the city and county superintendents of schools throughout the area.

In June 1971, this health advisory system was expanded to include CO (40 ppm, instantaneous) and NO_x (1.5 ppm, instantaneous). The purpose of the system was to enable students to curtail strenuous activities with the onset of moderately high air pollution levels and to warn persons having cardiac, respiratory diseases, or other air pollution sensetivities so that they may take precautions to protect themselves. On March 28, 1974, a new system, the "Emergency Contingency Plan (Regulation VII)" was adopted; it incorporated the part of the instantaneous criteria of the old system but added new levels for 1-hour and 24-hour averaging times. The new Stage 1 Episode replaces the function of School and Health Smog Warning health advisory. Including the new, lower levels for the 1-hour averaging times in the system has increased the number of times for which health advisories (Stage 1 Episodes) for ozone are reached. In the 6-month period between April 1 and September 30, there were 83 days with Stage 1 Episodes -- one-fourth of the year -- and no days having Stage 2 or Stage 3 episodes.

MONITORING INFORMATION

Continuous monitoring network covering 13 "air monitoring zones" in Los Angeles County

REPORTING FREQUENCY

Reported only when stated levels are exceeded

LENGTH OF TIME IN USE Adopted March 28, 1975. Replaces previous system operating for 20 years

INDEX ANALYSIS RECORD

LOCATION

San Francisco, California

AGENCY

Bay Area Air Pollution Control District
939 Ellis Street
San Francisco, California 94109

PHONE

(415)771-6000

		VARIABLES				**CLASSIFICATION**
☐ STATE	**AGENCY SIZE**	☒ CO	☒ NO_2	☐ PARTICULATE	☐ PART. SCATTER	
	220					$4D_2C$
☒ CITY		☐ SO_2	☒ O_3	☒ COH	☐ VISIBILITY	

CATEGORIES

Oxidant, ppm	CO, ppm	NO_2, ppm	COH units	Air Pollution Level
0.0-.05	0- 5	0.0-0.1	0.0-.05	Clean Air
.06-.09	6-10	.11-.14	0.6-1.5	Light
.10-.15	11-15	.15-.20	1.6-2.5	Significant
.16-.25	16-20	.21-.30	2.6-3.5	Heavy
>.25	> 20	> .30	>3.5	Severe
>.60	>100	>1.6	> 10	Emergency

RANGE

Actual Concentrations

EQUATION

N/A

DESCRIPTION

Data and categories are reported separately for each of 11 air monitoring stations. Categories are based on the highest value attained prior to 4:00 P.M. each day. Categories are specified for all four pollutants, and the maximum category becomes the overall designation for the air monitoring station. "For example: If San Jose shows an oxidant of 0.07 parts per million (light air pollution), and a coefficient of haze of 2.7 (heavy air pollution), the designation for San Jose will be heavy air pollution." [Air Currents, Vol. 15, No. 4, April 1972, p. 3.]

The current system, which was adopted in April 1972, emphasizes the maximum values; in 1968, however, the Agency began operating a Combined Pollutant Index (CPI) with five descriptor categories:

$$CPI = 2(O_x) + (NO_2) + (CO) + 10 \ (COH)$$

0- 25	Clean Air
26- 50	Light Air Pollution
51- 75	Moderate Air Pollution
76-100	Heavy Air Pollution
>101	Severe Air Pollution

This index was computed separately for three geographical areas -- north, central, and south. This combined index was replaced by the current one because it sometimes led to public confusion. Combining the four pollutants often created ambiguity -- at the Livermore station, for example, the federal oxidant standard might be violated for 100 days in a given year accompanied by low values for the other air pollutants; the resulting index would appear low, however. Conversely, high values sometimes were observed at the San Francisco station even though no standard was violated, giving misleading values.

MONITORING INFORMATION

11 full continuous air monitoring stations

REPORTING FREQUENCY

Forecast at 9:30 A.M.
Actual values at
4:30 P.M.

LENGTH OF TIME IN USE

Begun in Oct. 1968
Replaced in April
1972

INDEX ANALYSIS RECORD

LOCATION	AGENCY		
Denver, Colorado	State of Colorado Department of Health 4210 East 11th Avenue Denver, Colorado 80220		CLASSIFICATION

PHONE

(303)388-6111

	AGENCY SIZE	VARIABLES			CLASSIFICATION
☐ STATE ☒ CITY	54	☒ CO ☐ SO$_2$ ☐ NO$_2$ ☐ O$_3$ ☐ PARTICULATE ☒ COH ☐ PART. SCATTER ☐ VISIBILITY			2B$_2$C

CATEGORIES

CO, ppm	COH	Assigned Number	Color Code	Descriptor
<10	<1.0	1	Green	Good
10-19	1.0-1.9	2	Yellow	Good
20-29	2.0-2.9	3	Blue	Fair
30-39	3.0-3.9	4	Orange	Fair
40+	4.0+	5	Red	Poor

RANGE

1-5+

EQUATION

N/A

DESCRIPTION

The Denver Air Quality Index (DAQI) consists of two separate parts: an air quality index forecast and an air pollution dispersal index. The air quality index forecast is issued for the pollutant which has the highest assigned number. This number is determined by comparing the hourly average concentration for each pollutant with trend data for the same time period (monthly plots of the four-year average pollutant concentration for each hour of the day). Based on the comparison, an index forecast is made for the next three-hour period. The index may be updated hourly if significant changes are predicted.

The air pollution dispersal index is issued each morning and covers four time periods: A.M. today, P.M. today, A.M. tomorrow, and P.M. tomorrow. The index is the product of the wind speed (meters/second) and the mixing depth (hundreds of meters). The index categories and respective values are:

Bad	0/100 to 19/100
Fair	20/100 to 39/100
Good	40/100 to 59/100
Excellent	60/100 to 100/100

The air pollution index forecast is issued both as a number and a color; the number is displayed on a downtown bank sign, and, the number and color are displayed on a local freeway sign. The air pollution dispersal index is released to the local news media.

MONITORING INFORMATION	REPORTING FREQUENCY	LENGTH OF TIME IN USE
Monitoring data for index comes from one downtown station	Hourly as required	2 1/2 Years (Adopted July 1972)

INDEX ANALYSIS RECORD

LOCATION

Connecticut

PHONE

(203) 566-4030

AGENCY

Department of Environmental Protection
Air Compliance Section
165 Capitol Avenue
Hartford, Connecticut 06115

AGENCY SIZE

105

[X] STATE

[ ] CITY

VARIABLES

[ ] CO [ ] NO_2 [ ] PARTICULATE [ ] PART. SCATTER

[X] SO_2 [X] O_3 [X] COH [ ] VISIBILITY

CLASSIFICATION

$3D_1C$

CATEGORIES

O_3, ppm

0.000-0.04	Good
0.041-0.08	Satisfactory
0.081-0.20	Unsatisfactory
0.201-0.40	Unhealthy
0.401+	Harmful

RANGE

Actual Concentrations

EQUATION

N/A

DESCRIPTION

The index report gave the previous day's maximum one-hour ozone concentration and a forecast for the expected afternoon category. Before it was discontinued, a summer ozone index was reported in four cities listed in Table 5. Each daily index report gave the previous day's maximum one-hour ozone concentration and category, and the projected maximum one-hour ozone category for the afternoon. On Friday a similar report was issued with the projected maximum one-hour ozone category for Saturday. A similar type index was planned but not started for SO_2 and COH. The Agency is presently considering the adoption of a new index.

MONITORING INFORMATION

One continuous telemetered stations in each of the four cities.

REPORTING FREQUENCY

10:30 A.M. Daily,
3 P.M. Friday

LENGTH OF TIME IN USE

6 Months
Discontinued in 1973

INDEX ANALYSIS RECORD

LOCATION

Jacksonville, Florida

PHONE

(904)633-3303

AGENCY

Department of Health, Welfare, & Bio-Environmental Services
Bio-Environmental Services Division
Air and Water Pollution Control
515 West 6th Street
Jacksonville, Florida 32202

CLASSIFICATION

$6C_3C$

	AGENCY SIZE	VARIABLES			
☐ STATE		[X] CO	[X] NO_2	[X] PARTICULATE	☐ PART. SCATTER
[X] CITY	15	[X] SO_2	[X] O_3	[X] COH	☐ VISIBILITY

CATEGORIES

None

RANGE

Actual Concentrations

EQUATION

$$I = \frac{1}{6} \sum_{i=1}^{6} A_i; \quad A_i = 100 \frac{C_i}{S_i}$$

C_i = concentration of pollutant i

S_i = air quality standard for pollutant i

DESCRIPTION

The concentration of each of six air pollutants is reported as a function of the percent of the federal air quality standard; the average of these values also is reported. Thus, for each day, A_i is reported, along with I. The air quality standards used in the calculation are as follows:

Pollutant	S_i	Averaging Time (hrs.)
CO	9.0 ppm	8
SO_2	0.14 ppm	24
COH	3.0 units*	8
NO_2	0.20 ppm*	24
TSP	260 $\mu g/m^3$	24
Ozone	0.08 ppm	1

*Unofficial Standard

Because concentrations observed at different stations are not the same, the station whose daily concentrations are highest is selected for use in computing the index.

MONITORING INFORMATION

2 full continuous monitoring stations; 1 continuous oxidant station; 12 sequential stations which measure SO_2, NO_2, and TSP

REPORTING FREQUENCY

Daily, Including Sunday

LENGTH OF TIME IN USE

2 1/2 Years

INDEX ANALYSIS RECORD

LOCATION

Miami, Florida

PHONE

(305)635-7524

AGENCY

Metropolitan Dade County Pollution Control
864 N.W. 23rd Street
Miami, Florida 33127

AGENCY SIZE

50

	STATE
X	CITY

VARIABLES

X CO	X NO$_2$	☐ PARTICULATE	☐ PART. SCATTER		
☐ SO$_2$	X O$_3$	X COH	X VISIBILITY		

CLASSIFICATION

$5C_3C$

CATEGORIES

0- 20	Good
20- 40	Normal
40- 60	Moderate
60- 80	Heavy
80-100	Severe

RANGE

0-100+

EQUATION

$$I = \sum_{i=1}^{5} A_i$$

A_i = subindex obtained as described below.

DESCRIPTION

The air quality index is computed from five subindices. Each subindex is obtained by assigning subindex values for particular ranges of pollutant concentrations. Individual desciptors also are given to each of the subindices:

CO, ppm	NO$_2$, ppm	Oxidant, ppm	COH, units	Descriptor	Subindex, A_i
0- 1	0-.005	0-.005	0-0.5	Light	2
1- 2	.005-.01	.005-.01	0.5-1	Light	4
2- 4	.01-.02	.01-.04	1-2	Normal	8
4- 6	.02-.06	.04-.06	2-3	Moderate	12
6- 8	.06-.10	.06-.09	3-4	Heavy	**
8-35	.10-.20	.09-.10	4-5	Severe	**

Visibility, miles	Descriptor	Subindex, A_i
7-15 (No smoke or haze)	Good	2
7-15 (Little haze or smoke)	Good	4
4- 6 (Smoke or haze)	Poor	8
2- 4 (Smoke or haze)	Bad	12
1- 2 (Smoke or haze)	Very Bad	**
0- 1 (Smoke or haze)	Severe	**

**When values occur in these ranges, the staff is required to notify the "Chief of Evaluation" and to "continue to make hourly analyses of specific pollutants until concentrations are 'normal' again for two hours." Values assigned by Chief of Evaluation are ≥ 12.

MONITORING INFORMATION

Index is calculated from concentrations at one air monitoring station only (864 N.W. 23rd Street, Miami).

REPORTING FREQUENCY

Daily (weekdays only). Calculated at 9 A.M.

LENGTH OF TIME IN USE

2 1/2 Years

INDEX ANALYSIS RECORD

LOCATION

Tampa, Florida

PHONE

(813) 223-1311

AGENCY

Hillsborough County Environmental Protection Commission
305 North Morgan Street
Stovall Professional Building – Sixth Floor
Tampa, Florida   33602

☐ STATE	**AGENCY SIZE**
☒ CITY/COUNTY	16

VARIABLES

☒ CO   ☒ NO_2 ☐ PARTICULATE   ☐ PART. SCATTER

☒ SO_2 ☒ O_3 ☒ COH   ☐ VISIBILITY

CLASSIFICATION

$5A_3A$

CATEGORIES

0–19	Light
20–39	Moderate
40–49	Heavy
60–79	Very Heavy
80–99	Extremely Heavy
100+	Acute

RANGE

0–100+

EQUATION

$$ORAQI = \left[5.7 \sum_{i=1}^{5} (C_i/S_i) \right]^{1.37}$$

DESCRIPTION

The Agency uses the Oak Ridge Air Quality Index (ORAQI) described in Chapter VI, Section 2, except that CO is not being measured at the present time, but this appears to be temporary. The average concentration for each variable is calculated for the 24-hour period running from 8 A.M. to 8 A.M. each day. Each pollutant is weighted in the index according to its toxicological effect on humans, as indicated by the ORAQI nomograms.

MONITORING INFORMATION

Index is based on data from 2 continuous air monitoring stations.

REPORTING FREQUENCY

8 A.M. Daily

LENGTH OF TIME IN USE

3 Years

INDEX ANALYSIS RECORD

LOCATION	AGENCY
Atlanta, Georgia	Fulton County Health Department
PHONE	99 Butler Street, S.E.
(404)572-2846	Atlanta, Georgia 30303

	AGENCY SIZE	VARIABLES			CLASSIFICATION
☐ STATE	14	☒ CO ☐ NO$_2$ ☒ PARTICULATE ☐ PART. SCATTER			$3C_3C$
☒ CITY		☒ SO$_2$ ☐ O$_3$ ☐ COH ☐ VISIBILITY			

CATEGORIES

None

RANGE

0-100+

EQUATION

$$API = \frac{1}{3}\left(\frac{[PM]}{150} + \frac{[SO_2]}{315} + \frac{[CO]}{17}\right) \times 100$$

DESCRIPTION

The Air Pollution Index (API) is calculated as the average of the sum of three pollutant concentration:standard ratios using the criteria shown below. The average is then multiplied by 100 to give an index value of 100 when all pollutants are equal to their respective criteria. Thus, at index values above 100 "adverse effects could begin to be felt" while cleaner air would be indicated by lower values.

Pollutant	Averaging Time (hrs.)	1970 Federal Criteria
Suspended Particulate Matter [PM]	24	150 $\mu g/M^3$
[SO$_2$]	24	315 $\mu g/M^3$
[CO]	24	17 mg/M^3

Although, the agency does not define any descriptor categories for the index values, the two television stations which use the index have developed a common system of categories and descriptors for display purposes.

MONITORING INFORMATION	REPORTING FREQUENCY	LENGTH OF TIME IN USE
Index concentrations obtained from one "representative" station.	3 P.M. Daily	5 Years (Initiated in 1970)

INDEX ANALYSIS RECORD

LOCATION	AGENCY
Louisville, Kentucky	Air Pollution Control District of Jefferson County

PHONE

(502) 635-7471

Air Pollution Control District of Jefferson County
400 Reynolds Building
2500 South Third Street
Louisville, Kentucky 40208

	AGENCY SIZE	VARIABLES					CLASSIFICATION
☐ STATE	39	☒ CO	☒ NO_2	☐ PARTICULATE	☐ PART. SCATTER		$5C_3B$
☒ CITY		☒ SO_2	☒ O_3	☒ COH	☐ VISIBILITY		

CATEGORIES

0-30	Good
31-60	Acceptable
61-90	Unsatisfactory
90+	Unhealthy

RANGE

0-90+

EQUATION

$$I = \sum_{i=1}^{5} K_i C_i$$

Weighting factors K_i are determined as indicated below.

DESCRIPTION

Weighting factors for use in the equation are as follows:

i	Pollutant	Units	Averaging Time (hrs.)	K_i
1	CO	ppm	4	3.07
2	NO_2	ppm	4	267
3	SO_2	ppm	8	267
4	Ozone	ppm	4	533
5	COH	units	4	16.7

Thus, the index is calculated as: $I = 3.07(CO) + 267(NO_2) + 267(SO_2) + 533(O_3) + 16.7(COH)$

The weighting factors K_i relate primarily to short-term primary (health effect) standards. Descriptor categories are defined as follows:

Good: "All pollutant levels are below the numerical value for the annual standards."

Acceptable: "One or more of the pollutants are above the annual standard, but yet at a level such that the standard can be met unless the level persists for an extended period of time."

Unsatisfactory: "One or more of the pollutants is at a level such that if the level persists, the annual standard will not be met."

Unhealthy: "One or more of the pollutants is at such a level that health effects may occur after prolonged exposure. One or more of the pollutants may be exceeding short-term standards. One or more of the pollutants may have reached or may be approaching the 'Alert' level specified in the Episode Control Regulation."

The current index was adopted in October 1972. It replaced an earlier index initiated in 1970 which contained only two pollutants -- SO_2 and COH -- and which used the same computation procedure but with slightly different weighting factors.

Example of Report: "Afternoon Pollutant Index: 77; Problem Pollutant: Ozone; Primary Source: Vehicular Exhaust; The ozone levels were elevated during the afternoon, but did not remain below the unhealthy level."

MONITORING INFORMATION	REPORTING FREQUENCY	LENGTH OF TIME IN USE
Not Available	9:00 A.M. and 3:00 P.M. Daily	Initiated Oct. 1972 replacing an index started in 1970

INDEX ANALYSIS RECORD

LOCATION	AGENCY
Baltimore, Maryland	Maryland State Department of Health and Mental Hygiene
	Bureau of Air Quality Control
PHONE	610 N. Howard Street
(301) 383-2042	Baltimore, Maryland 21202

AGENCY SIZE	VARIABLES			CLASSIFICATION
	☐ STATE [X] CITY	90	[X] CO ☐ PARTICULATE [X] SO_2 [X] COH	[X] NO_2 ☐ PART. SCATTER [X] O_3 ☐ VISIBILITY	$5B_2B$

CATEGORIES

0- 24	Good
25- 49	Fair
50- 74	Poor
75- 99	Very Poor
100-249	Hazardous
250-749	Dangerous
750-999	Emergency
1000+	Endangerment

RANGE

0-1000+

EQUATION

N/A

DESCRIPTION

The Maryland Elevated Pollutant Index used in Baltimore County is very similar to the index used in the Washington, D.C. region. The Maryland Index is calculated using the following table which is based on the NAAQS and Federal Episode Criteria:

Index Breakpoints

Maryland Standard	$\underline{K}$	CO ppm	SO_2 ppm	COH ___	NO_2 ppm	OX ppm
More Adverse	25	20	0.10	1.75	0.25	0.04
Serious	50	35	0.20	3.00	0.40	0.08
Alert	100	60	0.70	5.50	0.60	0.10
Warning	250	90	1.40	9.20	1.2	0.40
Emergency	750	110	1.85	12.8	1.6	0.60
Endangerment	1000	125	2.33	14.6	2.0	0.70

The 1-hour averages (where standard do not exist) are based on correlation analysis relating the concentrations for the NAAQS averaging time to the concentrations at a 1-hour averaging time.

For each of the five pollutants, the above breakpoints (K and its corresponding concentration) are coordinates of a segmented linear function intercepting the origin, as discussed in Chapter VI, Section 2. Each of the five curves gives a pollutant subindex; the maximum subindex is reported as the daily index for Baltimore County.

MONITORING INFORMATION	REPORTING FREQUENCY	LENGTH OF TIME IN USE
Not Available	9:15 A.M. and 2:15 P.M.	2 Years

INDEX ANALYSIS RECORD

LOCATION	AGENCY
Detroit, Michigan	Wayne County Department of Health
PHONE	Air Pollution Control Division
(313)224-4650	1311 East Jefferson
	Detroit, Michigan 48207

	AGENCY SIZE	VARIABLES				CLASSIFICATION
☐ STATE	77	☐ CO	☐ NO₂	☐ PARTICULATE	☐ PART. SCATTER	1A₁C
☒ CITY		☐ SO₂	☐ O₃	☒ COH	☐ VISIBILITY	

CATEGORIES

M.U.R.C. Index	Degree of Dirtiness
0 - 30	Extremely light contamination
31 - 60	Light contamination
61 - 90	Medium contamination
91 - 120	Heavy contamination
121 and over	Extremely heavy contamination

RANGE

0-121+

EQUATION

$$M.U.R.C. = 70(COH)^{0.7}$$

DESCRIPTION

M.U.R.C. - pronounced "murk" - is an acronym which means Measure of Undesirable Respirable Contaminants. The M.U.R.C. index values reflect an approximation of the actual concentration of suspended particulate matter in the air. A range of M.U.R.C. values from 30 to 120 by the above equation equals a COH range of 0.3 to 2.15. This range is approximately equal to 35 to 350 micrograms/cubic meter. However, for M.U.R.C. values higher than 120, the correlation with suspended particulate matter concentration does not hold.

The morning report includes the index for Detroit together with the previous day's 24-hour average, maximum, and minimum values. These values are transmitted by telephone to the major newspapers and National Weather Service teletype. The afternoon report includes the Detroit index and, on a rotating basis, an index from one of the 13 monitoring stations. These values are transmitted to the National Weather Service and one television station.

The M.U.R.C. index is also used in Memphis, Tennessee.

MONITORING INFORMATION	REPORTING FREQUENCY	LENGTH OF TIME IN USE
13 station telemetered network	8 A.M. and 4 P.M.	7 Years

INDEX ANALYSIS RECORD

LOCATION

Minnesota

PHONE

(612)296-7373

AGENCY

Minnesota Pollution Control Agency
Division of Air Quality
1935 W. County Road, B2
Roseville, Minnesota 55113

AGENCY SIZE

37

VARIABLES

[X] CO   [ ] NO_2 [X] PARTICULATE   [ ] PART. SCATTER

[X] SO_2 [ ] O_3 [ ] COH   [ ] VISIBILITY

CLASSIFICATION

$3A_3B$

CATEGORIES

APEX	SO_2, ppb	CO, ppm	PM, $\mu g/m^3$	
0- 20	0- 20	0-3	0- 60	Good
21-100	21-100	4-9	61-150	Satisfactory
101-155	101-140	10+	151-260	Unsatisfactory
155+	141+	10+	261+	Unhealthy

RANGE

0-155+

EQUATION

$$APEX = \left[9.58 \left(\frac{C_{SO_2}}{100} + \frac{C_{CO}}{9} + \frac{C_{PM}}{150} \right) \right]^{1.37}$$

DESCRIPTION

The Minnesota Air Pollution Index (APEX) operates in the four cities shown in Chapter V (Table 5). For each city, APEX is calculated using the city-wide average concentrations for each pollutant (if more than one monitoring station exists) for the 24-hour period ending at 2 P.M. The APEX equation is identical to the Oak Ridge Air Quality Index, with a coefficient of 9.58. This coefficient was chosen to give APEX a value of 100 when the concentrations of all three pollutants are equal to their secondary NAAQS. The following terms are included in the equation:

C_{SO_2} : The 24-hour average concentration of SO_2 in ppb; this value is divided by the secondary NAAQS 24-hour standard of 100 ppb (Note: this is the 1971 standard).

C_{CO} : The maximum eight-hour average concentration of CO in ppm; this value is divided by the secondary NAAQS eight-hour standard of 9 ppm.

C_{PM} : The 24-hour concentration of total suspended particulate matter in in $\mu g/m^3$; this value is divided by the secondary NAAQS 24-hour standard of 150 ug/m^3.

In addition to reporting the calculated APEX value, the actual concentrations for each pollutant are reported. These values are reported on "Air Quality Clocks," which are divided into categories based on the primary and secondary NAAQS:

APEX   Actual Concentrations

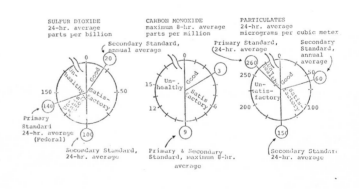

MONITORING INFORMATION

Minneapolis-St. Paul -- three continuous monitoring stations
Duluth -- one monitoring station
Rochester -- one monitoring station

REPORTING FREQUENCY

4 P.M. Daily

LENGTH OF TIME IN USE

3 Years

INDEX ANALYSIS RECORD

LOCATION	AGENCY
New Jersey	New Jersey Bureau of Air Pollution Control
PHONE	Division of Environmental Quality
(609)292-5450	Department of Environmental Protection
	P. O. Box 1390
	Trenton, New Jersey 08625

AGENCY SIZE 170

VARIABLES

[X] CO [ ] NO$_2$ [ ] PARTICULATE [ ] PART. SCATTER

[X] SO$_2$ [X] O$_3$ [X] COH [ ] VISIBILITY

[X] STATE [ ] CITY

CLASSIFICATION 4D$_1$A

CATEGORIES

CO, mg/m^3	SO$_2$, μg/m^3	COH	O$_3$, μg/m^3	
0- 3	0- 60	0- 60	0- 40	Good
3-15	60-260	60-150	40-130	Satisfactory
15-40	260-365	150-260	130-160	Unsatisfactory
40+	365+	260+	160+	Unhealthful

RANGE Actual Concentrations

EQUATION N/A

DESCRIPTION

The New Jersey Air Quality Index operates in the 20 cities listed in Chapter V (Table 5). The index reports actual concentrations "rather than arbitrary index numbers." For the 24-hour period ending at 2 P.M. daily, the Index reports the maximum 1-hour average concentration for CO and O$_3$ and the 24-hour average for SO$_2$ and COH. These units and time periods were chosen so the Index levels could be compared with the NAAQS for each pollutant. The index for each pollutant is displayed on an "Air Quality Clock" with the appropriate category divisions as shown below:

HOW THE NEW JERSEY AIR QUALITY INDEX RELATES TO NATIONAL AIR QUALITY STANDARDS

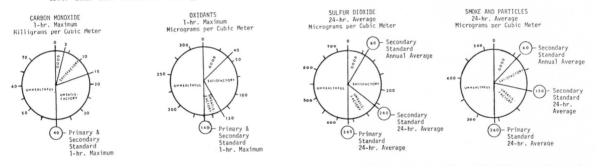

Clock faces show national primary and secondary air quality standards for sulfur dioxide, smoke and particles, carbon monoxide, and oxidants, as well as verbal ratings for pollutant levels to be used in the New Jersey Air Quality Index proposed by the Bureau of Air Pollution Control.

The Index falls in the "Unhealthful" category when the primary NAAQS for the pollutant has been exceeded at any time during the 24-hour period. The other categories are determined on the basis of the secondary NAAQS (for SO$_2$ and COH), mathematically (for CO), or empirically (for O$_3$), based on studies cited in the Federal Air Quality Criteria documents. The "Good", "Satisfactory", and "Unsatisfactory" categories are reached as the contaminant levels become increasingly higher but are still under the primary NAAQS.

In addition to the four individual indices, an overall daily rating is given for each city. This rating is a one-word summary based on the highest rating reached by any pollutant on that day.

MONITORING INFORMATION	REPORTING FREQUENCY	LENGTH OF TIME IN USE
18 continuous telemetered monitoring stations, four continuous comprehensive monitoring laboratories, covering 20 sities in all.	2 P.M. Daily	Adopted May 15, 1972

INDEX ANALYSIS RECORD

LOCATION
New York

PHONE
(518)457-7456

AGENCY
New York State Department of Environmental Conservation
50 Wolf Road
Albany, New York 12201

AGENCY SIZE
237

[X] STATE	
[ ] CITY	

VARIABLES

[X] CO	[ ] NO_2	[ ] PARTICULATE	[ ] PART. SCATTER	
[X] SO_2	[ ] O_3	[X] COH	[ ] VISIBILITY	

CLASSIFICATION
$3D_1A$

CATEGORIES

CO, ppm	SO_2, ppm	COH	Index Rating
0.0- 4.9	0.0 -0.02	0.0-0.3	Low
5.0-15.0	0.03-0.08	0.4-0.7	Medium
>15.0	>0.08	>0.7	High

RANGE
Actual Concentrations

EQUATION
N/A

DESCRIPTION

The New York State Index operates in the 11 localities shown in Chapter V (Table 5). Index ratings are calculated daily for each location:

Morning Index Rating : based on the 24-hour average pollutant concentrations period ending at midnight.

Noon Index Rating   : based on the 24-hour averages for the period ending at noon.

Forecast Index Rating : based on the Morning and Noon Index Ratings, the Index Forecast Rating is issued at 3 P.M. for the 24-hour period beginning at midnight.

Afternoon Index Rating: based on the 24-hour averages for the period ending at 2 P.M.

The Index Rating categories are based on the New York State Ambient Air Quality Standards:

Low   : concentrations in the lower half of standards

Medium : concentrations in the upper half of standards

High   : concentrations exceed standards

MONITORING INFORMATION
11 State-wide continuous telemetered monitoring stations

REPORTING FREQUENCY
3 P.M. Daily

LENGTH OF TIME IN USE
5 Years
(Initiated in late 1970)

INDEX ANALYSIS RECORD

LOCATION

New York, New York

PHONE

(212)566-5913

AGENCY

Department of Air Resources
Environmental Protection Administration
City of New York
51 Astor Place
New York, New York 10013

CLASSIFICATION

$5D_2A$

AGENCY SIZE

382

VARIABLES

[X] CO   [X] NO_2 [ ] PARTICULATE   [ ] PART. SCATTER

[X] SO_2 [X] O_3 [X] COH   [ ] VISIBILITY

[ ] STATE

[X] CITY

CATEGORIES

CO, ppm (8-hr.)	SO_2, ppm (24-hr.)	COH*	NO_2, ppm (24-hr.)	Ox, ppm (1-hr.)	
–	0–0.03	0–0.5	0–0.05	–	Good
–	0.04–0.06	0.5–1.0	0.06–0.09	–	Acceptable
–	0.07–0.10	1.1–1.6	0.10–0.12	–	Unsatisfactory
>9.0	>0.10	>1.6	>0.12	>0.08	Unhealthy

*Values for winter categories, summer values are 0.1 COH less

RANGE

Actual Concentrations

EQUATION

N/A

DESCRIPTION

   The Overall Air Quality Index is the one-word descriptor for the highest severity category reached by any one of the five pollutants.

MONITORING INFORMATION

11 continuous monitoring stations

REPORTING FREQUENCY

Daily

LENGTH OF TIME IN USE

4 Years

INDEX ANALYSIS RECORD

LOCATION

Ohio

PHONE

(614)469-3543

AGENCY

Ohio Environmental Protection Agency
361 East Broad Street
Columbus, Ohio 43216

AGENCY SIZE

228

CLASSIFICATION

$5B_2B$

VARIABLES

[X] CO	[X] NO_2	[X] PARTICULATE
		[ ] PART. SCATTER
[X] SO_2	[X] O_3	[ ] COH
		[ ] VISIBILITY

CATEGORIES

0- 40	Excellent		126-150	Poor
41- 60	Very Good		151-175	Very Poor
61- 80	Good		176-199	Extremely Poor
81- 99	Fair		200	Alert
100	Clean Air Std.		300	Warning
101-125	Unsatisfactory		400	Emergency

RANGE

0-400+

EQUATION

N/A

DESCRIPTION

The Ohio Air Quality Index is used in 13 cities within the State (Chapter V, Table 5). The index is calculated using the following table, which is based on the NAAQS and Federal Episode Criteria:

Index Breakpoints

	K	CO mg/M^3	SO_2 $\mu g/M^3$	PM $\mu g/M^3$	SO_2 x PM $(\mu g/M^3)^2$	NO_2 $\mu g/M^3$	NO_2 $\mu g/M^3$	Ox $\mu g/M^3$
Averaging Time (hrs.)	N/A	8	24	24	24	24	1	1
Ohio Air Quality Standard	100	10	260	150	–	–	–	119
Alert	200	17	800	375	65,000	282	1,130	200
Warning	300	34	1,600	625	261,000	565	2,260	800
Emergency	400	46	2,100	875	393,000	750	3,000	1,200

For each of five pollutants, the above breakpoints (K and its corresponding concentration) are the coordinates of a segmented linear function intercepting the origin, as discussed in Chapter VI, Section 2. Each of the five curves gives a pollutant subindex; the maximum subindex is reported as the daily index.

MONITORING INFORMATION

Varies from city to city

REPORTING FREQUENCY

Varies from city to city

LENGTH OF TIME IN USE

2 Years

(Adopted May 1973)

INDEX ANALYSIS RECORD

LOCATION

Oklahoma City, Oklahoma

PHONE

(405)427-8651

AGENCY

Oklahoma City County Health Department
Air Quality Control Section
921 NE 23rd Street
Oklahoma City Oklahoma 73105

CLASSIFICATION

$1A_1C$

AGENCY SIZE

15

☐ STATE	
☒ CITY	

VARIABLES

☐ CO		☐ NO_2		☐ PARTICULATE		☐ PART. SCATTER	
☐ SO_2		☐ O_3		☒ COH		☐ VISIBILITY	

CATEGORIES

M.U.R.C. Index	Degree of Dirtiness
0 - 30	Extremely light contamination
31 - 60	Light contamination
61 - 90	Medium contamination
91 - 120	Heavy contamination
121 and over	Extremely heavy contamination

RANGE

0-125+

EQUATION

$$M.U.R.C. = 70(COH)^{0.7}$$

DESCRIPTION

M.U.R.C. - pronounced "murk" - is an acronym which means Measure of Undesirable Respirable Contaminants. The M.U.R.C. index values reflect an approximation of the actual concentration of suspended particulate matter in the air. A range of M.U.R.C. values from 30 to 120 by the above equation equals a COH range of 0.3 to 2.15. This range is approximately equal to 35 to 350 micrograms/cubic meter. However, for M.U.R.C. values higher than 120 the correlation with suspended particulate matter concentration does not hold.

The M.U.R.C. index is currently used in Detroit, Michigan, and Memphis, Tennessee.

MONITORING INFORMATION

Not Available

REPORTING FREQUENCY

A.M. and P.M.

LENGTH OF TIME IN USE

2 1/2 Years
Discontinued in 1973

INDEX ANALYSIS RECORD

LOCATION	AGENCY
Portland, Oregon	Oregon State Department of Environmental Quality
PHONE	Air Quality Control Division
(503)229-5348	1234 S.W. Morrison
	Portland, Oregon 97205

AGENCY SIZE	VARIABLES				CLASSIFICATION
[X] STATE	[ ] CO	[ ] NO_2	[ ] PARTICULATE	[X] PART. SCATTER	$1D_1C$
20*					
[ ] CITY	[ ] SO_2	[ ] O_3	[ ] COH	[ ] VISIBILITY	

CATEGORIES	RANGE
Percent	0-100%
	EQUATION
0- 20 Very Light	
21- 40 Light	N/A
41- 70 Normal	
71- 90 Heavy	
91-100 Very Heavy	

DESCRIPTION

   The Agency's index, a "Pollution Particle Index," represents the relative percent of particulates in the air as measured by an instrument called the nephelometer. A normal day is considered to have a reference level of 50 based on 1973 data; B-scattering used to compute the index is based on the frequency distribution curve for 1973 data. The maximum 1-hour average value observed prior to 4:00 P.M. each day is used in computing the index. Fog or light rain do not affect the nephelometer, "which is specific for airborne particulate."

   Gaseous air contaminants are listed separately as maximum one-hour average values, along with reference data explaining the concentrations.

---
*
State Agency operates city air pollution control agency; estimate of staff includes portion of Agency manpower involved in immediate metropolitan area.

MONITORING INFORMATION	REPORTING FREQUENCY	LENGTH OF TIME IN USE
Index is based on one nephelometer site; other stations exist but do not have a nephelometer.	Once Daily at 4 P.M.	1/2 Year (Initiated in August 1974)

INDEX ANALYSIS RECORD

LOCATION

Philadelphia, Pennsylvania

PHONE

(215)686-7840

AGENCY

City of Philadelphia
Department of Public Health
Air Management Services
4320 Wissahickon Avenue
Philadelphia, Pennsylvania 19129

CLASSIFICATION

$2B_3C$

AGENCY SIZE	VARIABLES			
	☐ CO	☐ NO_2	☐ PARTICULATE	☐ PART. SCATTER
94	☒ SO_2	☐ O_3	☒ COH	☐ VISIBILITY

☐ STATE

☒ CITY

CATEGORIES

　　1 - 3　　　Below Average
　　4 - 6　　　Average
　　7 - 10　　Above Average

RANGE

1-10

EQUATION

$$I = \frac{I(SO_2) + I(COH)}{2}$$

DESCRIPTION

　　The air pollution information issued each day is based on the sulfur dioxide (SO_2) concentration and the smoke shade measured at 1501 E. Lycoming Street, the Air Management Services Laboratory. This station was chosen for its length of time as a continuous data producer. The forecast is issued twice daily and is based on the above mentioned pollutants measured during the early morning and mid-day hours, indicative of average conditions for the day. The forecast can be affected by changes in wind speed, wind direction, atmospheric inversions, and other weather parameters, as well as increased or reduced pollutant loading by industrial, automotive, and other community sources.

　　Both the forecast and index are based on frequency distributions of sulfur dioxide and smoke shade. The morning forecast is prepared by comparing the SO_2 concentration for the 10th hour of any day with a frequency distribution of past data broken down into class intervals which have been assigned values of 1 through 10. The same procedure is done to the 2-4 A.M. smoke shade level and a corresponding number of 1 to 10 assigned to it. The average of these two numbers is issued to the news media and others as the "Air Pollution Forecast" for the day. The actual index for the preceding day is computed by comparing the 24-hour averages of both SO_2 and smoke shade with frequency distributions of past data based on daily averages of these pollutants. Thus, the actual index for the previous day is given to the media at the same time a forecast is made. Both the forecast and index are related in that 1, 2, and 3 are considered low levels of pollution; 4, 5, and 6 are average levels; 7, 8, and 9 above average levels; and 10 is considered an adverse level. The 12th hour SO_2 concentration and the 6-8 A.M. smoke shade level are used to predict the afternoon forecast.

MONITORING INFORMATION	REPORTING FREQUENCY	LENGTH OF TIME IN USE
13 stations, 1 mobile van	11 A.M. and 4 P.M.	10 Years

INDEX ANALYSIS RECORD

<table>
<tr><td>LOCATION
Pittsburgh, Pennsylvania</td><td colspan="2">AGENCY
Allegheny County Health Department
Bureau of Air Pollution Control
301 39th Street
Pittsburgh, Pennsylvania 15201</td></tr>
<tr><td>PHONE
(412)681-9600</td><td></td><td></td></tr>
</table>

AGENCY SIZE	VARIABLES		CLASSIFICATION
	☐ CO ☐ NO_2 ☐ PARTICULATE ☐ PART. SCATTER		$2C_3B$
82	☒ SO_2 ☐ O_3 ☒ COH ☐ VISIBILITY		

☐ STATE   ☒ CITY

CATEGORIES

0- 15	Excellent
15- 35	Satisfactory
35-100	Unsatisfactory
100-200	Poor - First Stage Alert
200-250	Very Poor - Second Stage Alert
250+	Emergency - Emergency Stage

RANGE

0-250+

EQUATION

$$API = 50\left(\frac{[SO_2]}{0.14} + \frac{[COH]}{1.73}\right)$$

DESCRIPTION

The Air Pollution Index (API) equation includes:

$[SO_2]$: the 24-hour average SO_2 concentration (ppm)

0.14: the 24-hour Primary NAAQS for SO_2 (ppm)

$[COH]$: the 24-hour average coefficient of haze

1.73: the COH value equivalent to the Primary NAAQS of 260 $\mu g/m^3$ for particulate matter; in Allegheny County 1 COH = 150 $\mu g/m^3$

Although the onset of air pollution episodes is not based on API, the index can be correlated with the Allegheny County Episode Criteria. These criteria include the critical values of SO_2 and COH (or their product) coupled with at least 36 hours of air stagnation. Index values of 100, 200, and 250 approximately correspond to the Alert I, Alert II, and Emergency Episode stages.

API is reported seven days a week to the public and news media through separate telephone recordings (Codophone). The report includes the average index for the whole county, the index value at each monitoring location, and the average index for the previous 365 days.

MONITORING INFORMATION	REPORTING FREQUENCY	LENGTH OF TIME IN USE
Seven continuous monitoring stations	6:30 and 10:30 A.M. 5:30 and 10:30 P.M.	4 Years (Initiated in 1971)

INDEX ANALYSIS RECORD

LOCATION

Chatanooga, Tennessee

PHONE

(615)867-4321

AGENCY

Chatanooga-Hamilton County Air Pollution Control Bureau
3511 Rossville Boulevard
Chatanooga, Tennessee 37407

	AGENCY SIZE	VARIABLES						CLASSIFICATION
☐ STATE	22	☐ CO	☐ NO_2	☒ PARTICULATE	☐ PART. SCATTER			$1D_1C$
☒ CITY		☐ SO_2	☐ O_3	☐ COH	☐ VISIBILITY			

CATEGORIES

0- 70	$\mu g/m^3$	Light
75-130	$\mu g/m^3$	Moderate
130-200	$\mu g/m^3$	Heavy
>200	$\mu g/m^3$	Alert

RANGE

Actual Concentration

EQUATION

N/A

DESCRIPTION

This Agency's index reflects only particulate matter (as measured by high volume samplers). Sometimes another pollutant is also reported with the index if it exceeds a standard.

MONITORING INFORMATION

Index based on two hi-vol samplers at roof of main location. One runs 8 A.M. - 8 A.M.; the other runs 4 P.M. - 4 P.M.

REPORTING FREQUENCY

Twice Daily

LENGTH OF TIME IN USE

1 1/2 Years

INDEX ANALYSIS RECORD

LOCATION	AGENCY
Memphis, Tennessee	City of Memphis – Shelby Health Department
PHONE	814 Jefferson Avenue
(901)522-2736	Memphis, Tennessee 38105

AGENCY SIZE	VARIABLES				CLASSIFICATION
14	☐ CO	☐ NO$_2$	☐ PARTICULATE	☐ PART. SCATTER	1A$_1$C
	☐ SO$_2$	☐ O$_3$	☒ COH	☐ VISIBILITY	

☐ STATE ☒ CITY

CATEGORIES

M.U.R.C. Index	Degree of Dirtiness
0- 30	Extremely light contamination
31- 60	Light contamination
61- 90	Medium contamination
91-120	Heavy contamination

RANGE

0-120+

EQUATION

$$M.U.R.C. = 70(COH)^{0.7}$$

DESCRIPTION

This single-pollutant index, based on two-hour average COH readings, is the same as the M.U.R.C. index used in Oklahoma City, Oklahoma, and Detroit, Michigan. The Memphis M.U.R.C. is based on two-hour average COH readings. The M.U.R.C. index values reflect an approximation of the actual concentration of suspended particulate matter. Index values from 30 to 120 equals a range of 0.3 to 2.15 COH. This range is approximately equal to 35 to 350 micrograms/cubic meter. For M.U.R.C. values higher than 120, this correlation does not hold.

MONITORING INFORMATION	REPORTING FREQUENCY	LENGTH OF TIME IN USE
12 monitoring sites covering gases and particulate Index is based on one site that is centrally located in the urban area.	Daily, weekdays only: 10 A.M. and 4 P.M.	2 Years

INDEX ANALYSIS RECORD

LOCATION

Nashville, Tennessee

AGENCY

Metropolitan Health Department of Nashville and Davidson County
Bureau of Environmental Control
Pollution Control Division
311 23rd Avenue, North
Nashville, Tennessee 37203

PHONE

(615)327-9312

AGENCY SIZE	VARIABLES					CLASSIFICATION

☐ STATE

AGENCY SIZE: 17

X CITY

VARIABLES:
☐ CO ☐ NO_2 ☐ PARTICULATE ☐ PART. SCATTER
☐ SO_2 ☐ O_3 X COH ☐ VISIBILITY

CLASSIFICATION: $1C_1C$

CATEGORIES

0-25	Slight
26-50	Moderate
51-75	Heavy
>75	Extremely Heavy

RANGE

0-75+

EQUATION

$$I = 25(COH)$$

DESCRIPTION

The "Air Pollution Index" is based only on the soiling index (COH) and has four categories.

High-volume samplers measure particulate levels at 18 sites, but the index uses only the COH data from tape samplers operate at two sites. The index is computed from data for the 2-hour period from 6:00 A.M. - 8:00 A.M. Due to staffing limitations, the index is only estimated for Saturday and Sunday.

MONITORING INFORMATION

2 full continuous air monitoring stations (SO_2, NO_x, CO, O_3, COH); other measurements at 20 sites. Index is based on COH only which is measured at two sites.

REPORTING FREQUENCY

Daily, including Sat. and Sunday, at 8 A.M.

LENGTH OF TIME IN USE

5 Years (Initiated Jan. 1970)

INDEX ANALYSIS RECORD

LOCATION

Dallas, Texas

PHONE

(214)630-1111

AGENCY

City of Dallas Department of Public Health
Air Pollution Control Section
1500 W. Mockingbird Street
Dallas, Texas 75235

	AGENCY SIZE					CLASSIFICATION
☐ STATE		**VARIABLES**				
	21	☐ CO	☒ NO₂	☐ PARTICULATE	☒ PART. SCATTER	$2C_3B$
☒ CITY		☐ SO₂	☐ O₃	☐ COH	☐ VISIBILITY	

CATEGORIES

0-30	Light
31-60	Moderate
61-90	Heavy
>91	Severe

RANGE

0-91+

EQUATION

$$I = \frac{2(TSP) + NO_2}{10}$$

(24-hour averages)

DESCRIPTION

The formula results from a 6-month research study which was undertaken to determine how concentrations observed at two locations 5 miles apart -- the air pollution laboratory and downtown Dallas -- relate to each other. The study indicated that downtown particulate levels generally were two times those at the laboratory location, while NO_2 levels were approximately the same at both locations. Using these results, downtown levels could be estimated from measurements at the laboratory, and this fact was incorporated into the index. Thus, in computing the index, TSP and NO_2 are 24-hour average concentrations measured at the laboratory ($\mu g/m^3$), while the index reflects the downtown levels.

The index is released at 11:00 A.M. Monday through Friday along with a 24-hour forecast. The forecast is based on index level trends, projected meteorological conditions, and anticipated air pollution activities. The Friday forecast attempts to cover the weekend.

For index values greater than 66, the possibility exists for declaring the "Alert Level" for an air pollution episode, as defined by the Texas Air Pollution Control Board. The index value approaching 100 indicates that pollution levels are becoming high enough that, if they continue, a "Warning Level" may be declared.

MONITORING INFORMATION

Index is computed from one monitoring site equipped with high-volume sampler and NO_2 instrument.

REPORTING FREQUENCY

Once Daily at
11 A.M.

LENGTH OF TIME IN USE

2 1/2 Years

(Initiated Aug. 1972)

INDEX ANALYSIS RECORD

LOCATION

Seattle, Washington

AGENCY

Puget Sound Air Pollution Control Agency
410 West Harrison Street
Seattle, Washington   98119

PHONE

(206)344-7328

AGENCY SIZE

39

	VARIABLES		
☐ STATE	☐ CO	☐ NO_2	☐ PARTICULATE	☐ PART. SCATTER
☒ CITY	☒ SO_2	☐ O_3	☒ COH	☐ VISIBILITY

CLASSIFICATION

$2B_2B$

CATEGORIES

0- 50	Alert
50-100	Warning
100-150	Emergency

RANGE

0-150+

EQUATION

N/A

DESCRIPTION

The Puget Sound Air Quality Index is calculated using the following table, which is based on the stages of an Emergency Episode Plan:

Index Breakpoints

	K	SO_2, ppm (24-hr.)	COH (24-hr.)	SO_x x COH
Alert	50	0.3	3.0	0.2
Warning	100	0.6	5.0	0.8
Emergency	150	0.8	7.0	1.2

For each of the three pollutants, the above breakpoints (K and its corresponding concentration) are the coordinates of a segmented linear function intercepting the origin, as discussed in Chapter VI, Section 2. Each of the three curves gives a pollutant subindex; the maximum subindex is reported as the daily index.

MONITORING INFORMATION

10 air monitoring sites with data telemetered to a central computer

REPORTING FREQUENCY

3 times daily: morning, afternoon, and evening

LENGTH OF TIME IN USE

4 Years
(Initiated in 1971)

INDEX ANALYSIS RECORD

Washington, D.C.

PHONE

(202)347-4637

AGENCY

District of Columbia Department of Environmental Services
Bureau of Air and Water Pollution Control
614 H Street, N.W.
Washington, D.C.   20001

AGENCY SIZE	VARIABLES					CLASSIFICATION

AGENCY SIZE

14

VARIABLES

X	CO	X	NO_2	☐	PARTICULATE	☐	PART. SCATTER
X	SO_2	X	O_3	X	COH	☐	VISIBILITY

CLASSIFICATION

$5B_2B$

CATEGORIES

0- 24	Good
25- 49	Fair
50- 74	Poor
75- 99	Unhealthy
100-249	Hazardous
250-749	Dangerous
750+	Very Dangerous

RANGE

0-750+

EQUATION

N/A

DESCRIPTION

This index, which is operated by the Washington Metropolitan Council of Governments (COG) for the six jurisdictions in the Washington metropolitan area (Chapter V, Table 5), is very similar to the index used in Baltimore, Maryland, from which it was partially derived. The COG Index is calculated using the following table, which is based on the NAAQS and Federal Episode Criteria:

Index Breakpoints
(1-hour average concentrations)

	K	CO ppm	SO_2 ppm	COH	NO_2 ppm	OX ppm
Secondary NAAQS	25	20	0.10	1.75	0.25	0.04
Primary NAAQS	50	35	0.20	3.00	0.40	0.08
Alert	100	60	0.70	5.50	0.60	0.10
Warning	250	90	1.40	9.20	1.2	0.40
Emergency	750	110	1.85	12.8	1.6	0.60

The 1-hour criteria (where standards do not exist) are based on correlation analyses relating the concentrations at the NAAQS averaging time to the concentrations at a 1-hour averaging time.

For each of the five pollutants, the above breakpoints (K and its corresponding concentration) are coordinates of a segmented linear function intercepting the origin, as discussed in Chapter VI, Section 2. Each of the five curves gives a pollutant subindex; the maximum subindex is reported as the daily index for the region.

The index is made available twice daily to the news media through a telephone recording.

MONITORING INFORMATION

One station in each of the six jurisdictions

REPORTING FREQUENCY

9 A.M. and 3 P.M.
Daily

LENGTH OF TIME IN USE

1 1/2 Years

INDEX ANALYSIS RECORD

LOCATION	AGENCY
Alberta, Canada	Department of the Environment
PHONE	Environmental Protection Services
(403)427-5893	Division of Pollution Control
	Milner Building, 10040 - 104 Street
	Edmonton, Alberta T5J 0Z6

	AGENCY SIZE	VARIABLES					CLASSIFICATION
X STATE		X CO	X NO$_2$	☐ PARTICULATE	☐ PART. SCATTER		$5A_3C$
☐ CITY	26	X SO$_2$	X O$_3$	X COH	☐ VISIBILITY		

CATEGORIES

0- 25	Clean
26- 50	Light
51- 75	Moderate
76-100	Heavy
100+	Severe

RANGE

0-100+

EQUATION

$$I = OX^{1.3} + (0.5\ NO_x\ or\ NO_2) + CO^{1.05} + (10\ COH)^{1.2} + \left(\frac{SO_2}{3}\right)^{1.55}$$

DESCRIPTION

The Alberta Air Quality Index operates in the two cities shown in Chapter V, Table 6. As its author notes, "the intent of the Alberta index is to make the public aware of the general air quality. They should not associate a specific index level with a health hazard as the index was not designed to serve that purpose. [Our combined index] has the advantage of a single index number representing the five major pollutants but has the disadvantage of being unable to determine from the index value whether a specific pollutant is high or low. However, as the index is for information only and the Alberta alert plan will cover the situation of high individual pollutant levels, this is deemed to be an acceptable weakness."

The index is based on pollutant levels from a single monitoring station within each city. The index equation is designed so each pollutant contributes a value of 15 to the combined index at the following 1-hour air quality standards:

<u>1-hour standard</u>

CO	13	ppm
SO$_2$	17	pphm
Particulate Matter	0.9	COH
NO$_x$	30	pphm
NO$_2$	15	pphm
Oxidants	8	pphm

The resulting index equation is very sensitive to smoke levels (particulate matter) and oxidants, thereby reflecting the public concern with visibility and health effects. The index categories are based on those used in San Francisco prior to October 1968. Monthly mean and peak index values for Edmonton and Calgary are calculated and compared to meteorological and emission inventory data.

MONITORING INFORMATION	REPORTING FREQUENCY	LENGTH OF TIME IN USE
One station in each city	8 A.M. and 3 P.M. Daily	1 Year

LOCATION	AGENCY
Ontario, Canada	Air Management Branch
	Ministry of the Environment
PHONE	880 Bay Street
(416)965-6343	Toronto, Ontario M5S 1Z8

	AGENCY SIZE	VARIABLES				CLASSIFICATION
☒ STATE	70	☐ CO	☐ NO$_2$	☐ PARTICULATE	☐ PART. SCATTER	$2A_3B$
☐ CITY		☒ SO$_2$	☐ O$_3$	☒ COH	☐ VISIBILITY	

CATEGORIES	RANGE
	0-100+

CATEGORIES		EQUATION
0-31	Acceptable	
32-49	Advisory Level	
50-74	First Alert	$API = 0.2\,(30.5\,COH + 126.0\,SO_2)^{1.35}$
75-99	Second Alert	
100+	Episode Threshold Level	

DESCRIPTION

The Ontario Air Pollution Index (API) operates in six cities of the Province (Chapter V, Table 6). The data required to calculate the index are:

COH = 24-hour running average of the soiling index expressed as coefficient of haze per thousand linear feet.

SO_2 = 24-hour running average of sulfur dioxide concentrations in parts per million.

The coefficients and exponent of the API equation were derived by evaluating the concentration data for sulfur dioxide and suspended particulate matter from past air pollution episodes. An analysis of the data revealed the following pairs of values could be used as the threshold to a severe episode at which the Air Pollution Index is set to equal 100:

1. Suspended particulates 600 ug/m^3 which for Toronto is equivalent to 2.75 COH and sulphur dioxide .13 p.p.m.

2. Suspended particulates 500 ug/m^3 equivalent to 2.24 COH and sulphur dioxide .25 p.p.m.

Setting the equation for the Air Pollution Index as a function of the 24-hour average concentrations of SO_2 and COH as follows:

$$API = A(COH) + B(SO_2) \qquad (1)$$

and substituting the foregoing given pairs of values for average concentrations of COH and SO_2 at API equal to 100, gives the following equation:

$$API' = 30.5(COH + 126.0(SO_2) \qquad (2)$$

For a desirable scale the API was made to be an exponential function of API', that is,

$$API = C[API']^D \qquad (3)$$

$$API = C[30.5(COH) + 126.0(SO_2)]^D \qquad (4)$$

The levels of coefficient of haze and sulfur dioxide set by Ontario Regulations as objectives are 24-hour averages of COH at 1.0 and SO_2 at .10 p.p.m. Setting API = 32 at these levels provides a range of indices twice as great, that is, from 33 to 100, for control action to take place than for the range of acceptable levels, 0 to 32. Substituting API = 100 for levels of COH and SO_2 given above and API = 32 when COH = 1.0 and SO_2 = .10 equation (4) can be solved for C and D to give the equation for the Air Pollution Index for Toronto as follows:

$$API = .2[30.5(COH) + 126.0(SO_2)]^{1.35}$$

(Continued)

MONITORING INFORMATION	REPORTING FREQUENCY	LENGTH OF TIME IN USE
Several continuous telemetered monitoring stations	Daily	5 Years

INDEX ANALYSIS RECORD

LOCATION

Ontario, Canada (Cont'd)

AGENCY

PHONE

| STATE | | CITY | |

AGENCY SIZE

VARIABLES

☐ CO ☐ NO_2 ☐ PARTICULATE ☐ PART. SCATTER

☐ SO_2 ☐ O_3 ☐ COH ☐ VISIBILITY

CLASSIFICATION

CATEGORIES

RANGE

EQUATION

DESCRIPTION

An Air Pollution Index of less than 32 is considered acceptable. At these levels, concentrations of sulfur dioxide and particulates should have little or no effect on human health. At the Advisory Level at which the Air Pollution Index is equal to 32 and meteorological conditions are expected to remain adverse for at least six more hours, owners of significant sources of pollution in the community may be advised to make preparation for the curtailment of their operations.

The First Alert occurs when the Air Pollution Index reaches 50 and adverse weather is forecast to continue for at least six hours. The Minister may order major sources to curtail their activities. Studies have shown that at levels over 50, patients with chronic respiratory diseases may experience an accentuation in symptoms.

If the abatement action does not succeed in lowering the pollution levels and the Index rises to 75, the Second Alert is issued. The Minister may order sources to make further curtailment in operations. When the Index reaches 100, the Air Pollution Episode Threshold Level, the Minister may require the curtailment of all sources not essential to public health or safety. At this level, the air pollution could have mild effects on healthy people and might seriously endanger those with severe cardiac or respiratory disease.

MONITORING INFORMATION

REPORTING FREQUENCY

LENGTH OF TIME IN USE

AGENCIES USING INDICES

AGENCY NO. 1   AGENCY SIZE: 24   INDEX TYPE: $1D_1B$

We previously used the 4-stage alert system that was developed by the Los Angeles Air Pollution Control District 20 years ago. This was supplemented by a health advisory system designed to advise the most sensitive portion of the population. Now we are adopting an alert system that is based on the EPA federal episode warning system. We find that our community has become accustomed to the old 4-stage alert system, which was based on ozone, and the process of re-educating the public has been very difficult. They find the new episode warning system levels confusing, and the re-education process is a tremendous job. The news media, for example, still want to use the old terminology, which is inconsistent with the new episode terminology. The introduction, right now, of "an index would bury us."

AGENCY NO. 2   AGENCY SIZE: 380   INDEX TYPE: $3D_1B$

Previously, we used a health advisory system designed to warn school children and persons with respiratory illness and cardiac problems. We recently adopted a new episode system which has new levels for the various air pollutants and includes the old health advisory warning level as its Stage 1 Episode. With the new lower levels, there are more health advisory warnings (Stage 1 Episodes) than before. This created some public confusion initially. One of our problems is to get notification of adverse air pollution levels to the public, particularly to the schools, as quickly as possible. We are considering a new scheme in which a radio transmitter would transmit notification of an episode to radio receivers at each school.

---

*NOTE: THESE ARE INTERPRETATIONS BY THE INVESTIGATORS OF VIEWS EXPRESSED BY RESPONDENTS DURING TELEPHONE CONVERSATIONS.

AGENCIES USING INDICES (Cont'd)

AGENCY NO. 3   AGENCY SIZE: 220   INDEX TYPE: $4D_2B$

   Eight years ago we began using a combined air pollution index, which lumped CO, SO_2, and O_3 into one number. We found the use of such an index to be confusing to the public, and we abandoned it for a new approach in 1972. At one station, where CO and particulates were high while the other pollutants were low, we obtained misleadingly high index values. Conversely, at another station where the federal oxidant standard was exceeded frequently, while other pollutants were low, the net result was a misleadingly low index value. The combined index tended more to confuse the public than to clarify or communicate. We therefore abandoned the combined approach after four years and adopted a less misleading approach in which the highest concentrations determine the descriptor category reported for each air monitoring station.

AGENCY NO. 4   AGENCY SIZE: 54   INDEX TYPE: $2B_2C$

   The index we use originated in 1972 when a businessman offered to erect a sign on his building to give daily air quality readings. Response to this display sign has been so good that similar signs "should be placed all over the city." Our agency also prepares an air quality index forecast for use on a 24-hour telephone recording loop.

AGENCY NO. 5   AGENCY SIZE: 15   INDEX TYPE: $6C_3C$

   Our daily air pollution index has proved quite satisfactory. It covers six pollutants -- TSP, COH, CO, NO_2, SO_2, and O_3. The newspapers carry it daily, including Sunday, but most people probably don't see it.

---

*NOTE: THESE ARE INTERPRETATIONS BY THE INVESTIGATORS OF VIEWS EXPRESSED BY RESPONDENTS DURING TELEPHONE CONVERSATIONS.

AGENCIES USING INDICES (Cont'd)

AGENCY NO. 6   AGENCY SIZE: 50   INDEX TYPE: $5C_3C$

Our "pollution index," which has been in use for about 3 years, appears to be accepted well by the public. It is a combined index with 5 variables -- NO_2, CO, O_3, COH, and visibility factor. One problem with the index has to do with its lack of representativeness. Sometimes considerable pollution, such as heavy smoke, occurs in one part of the city, but, because we do not monitor there, our index does not reflect these levels. Thus our index does not adequately reflect the spatial variation in pollutant concentration. There is, perhaps, no way to make a perfect, all-purpose index.

AGENCY NO. 7   AGENCY SIZE: 14   INDEX TYPE: $3C_3C$

Established to maintain good public relations, the index has generated much interest. It is relayed to several radio and television stations and the Weather Bureau for dissemination to the public.

AGENCY NO. 8   AGENCY SIZE: 16   INDEX TYPE: $5A_3A$

We recently have begun using a "total air quality index" that is based on ORAQI. In general, we don't have much trouble explaining this index -- we provide a public information bulletin on the subject.

*NOTE: THESE ARE INTERPRETATIONS BY THE INVESTIGATORS OF VIEWS EXPRESSED BY RESPONDENTS DURING TELEPHONE CONVERSATIONS.

134

AGENCIES USING INDICES (Cont'd)

AGENCY NO. 9   AGENCY SIZE: 39   INDEX TYPE: $5C_3B$

Our air pollution index has great public interest, and it is reported by TV, the radio, and the newspaper. Our monitoring data are not as spatially representative as we would like them to, but that is a general problem with monitoring networks.

AGENCY NO. 10   AGENCY SIZE: 77   INDEX TYPE: $1A_1C$

The public can relate to this index more easily than to concentrations, since the scale is comparable to the Fahrenheit temperature scale.

AGENCY NO. 11   AGENCY SIZE: 13   INDEX TYPE: $3A_3B$

Once the public became familiar with the index, it proved useful. It now appears that people keep track of the change in the air quality category from day to day. However, the numbers resulting from the index calculation are not necessarily meaningful.

AGENCY NO. 12   AGENCY SIZE: 44   INDEX TYPE: $3D_1A$

In general, air quality indices are meaningless because they do not accurately reflect air quality. The data from which they are calculated is not representative of the region where the index is applicable.

AGENCY NO. 13   AGENCY SIZE: 37   INDEX TYPE: $3D_1A$

Indices are helpful to the public, since they allow the public to get a feeling about air quality. However, the layman does not understand the technical language of air pollution. Some people have asked us about the air quality of other cities before moving their home.

* NOTE: THESE ARE INTERPRETATIONS BY THE INVESTIGATORS OF VIEWS EXPRESSED BY RESPONDENTS DURING TELEPHONE CONVERSATIONS.

AGENCIES USING INDICES (Cont'd)

AGENCY NO. 14   AGENCY SIZE: 382   INDEX TYPE: $5D_2A$

Although indices do not tell the whole story about air pollution levels, they are useful in keeping the public aware of air quality. The many different indices in use make it difficult to compare them. Our index was not developed on any scientific basis and is not intended as such.

AGENCY NO. 15   AGENCY SIZE: 12   INDEX TYPE: $3D_1A$

Our index must not be that important to people because we have received no comments on it since it was established.

AGENCY NO. 16   AGENCY SIZE: 65   INDEX TYPE: $5B_2B$

We have received a good response to our index, which is reported on the local radio and television stations and in the newspapers. The index helps inform the public about air quality and pollutant-source relationships.

AGENCY NO. 17   AGENCY SIZE: 80   INDEX TYPE: $5B_2B$

Although initial public response to the index has been very good, people have become insensitive to it since the index exceeds 100 (the standard) most of the time. I question the validity of reporting only the index for the "dirtiest" part of the city, and I question representativeness for the region as a whole.

AGENCY NO. 18   AGENCY SIZE: 20   INDEX TYPE: $1D_1C$

Our index, a pollution particle index, was started just three weeks ago. It is based on measurements from the integrating nephelometer, which reflects the amount of light scattering from small particles, independent of humidity. We report the index once a day.

* NOTE: THESE ARE INTERPRETATIONS BY THE INVESTIGATORS OF VIEWS EXPRESSED BY RESPONDENTS DURING TELEPHONE CONVERSATIONS.

AGENCIES USING INDICES (Cont'd)

AGENCY NO. 19   AGENCY SIZE: 82   INDEX TYPE: $2C_3B$

We think our index is one of the best. It reports not only the major pollutants in both a separate and combined index, but the index values also are related to the air pollution episode program.

AGENCY NO. 20   AGENCY SIZE: 94   INDEX TYPE: $2B_3C$

Indices cannot describe the complete picture of the air quality and are useful only for indicating short-term and not the long-term air quality.

AGENCY NO. 21   AGENCY SIZE: 22   INDEX TYPE: $1D_1C$

Our index seems to work adequately. It gives people a feeling or a sense of how bad air pollution is on a daily basis. In the index, particulate matter alone (measured by the high-volume sampler) is reported; however, if ozone turns out to be high, we report that separately, as when we experience an air pollution alert

AGENCY NO. 22   AGENCY SIZE: 14   INDEX TYPE: $1A_1C$

Our index reports COH only, patterned after the index used in Detroit. We have discussed our index with the other air pollution control agencies, and we feel there is no one best index. Our index, which is usually published along with the weather report, seems to correlate well with public perception.

AGENCY NO. 23   AGENCY SIZE: 17   INDEX TYPE: $1C_1C$

Although we measure all six of the major air pollutants, we just report COH in our index, with the COH values multiplied by 25. We also report the pollen count for three monitoring stations.

*NOTE: THESE ARE INTERPRETATIONS BY THE INVESTIGATORS OF VIEWS EXPRESSED BY RESPONDENTS DURING TELEPHONE CONVERSATIONS.

AGENCIES USING INDICES (Cont'd)

AGENCY NO. 24   AGENCY SIZE: 21   INDEX TYPE: $2C_3B$

We based our index on a six-month research study in which we correlated the concentrations measured at a nearby location with those measured downtown. We found downtown particulate concentrations to be two times those at the reference location while NO_2 concentrations were approximately the same at both places. Now we predict the downtown values using only data from this reference location. Our combined index relates particulate and NO_2 concentrations to the Texas "alert" and "warning" episode levels. The index appears very accurate and is quite useful for the purpose for which it was intended.

AGENCY NO. 25   AGENCY SIZE: 39   INDEX TYPE: $2B_2B$

Our index was begun in 1971; before that we reported actual numerical measurements. The newspapers, however, wanted something more simple. Our index, which is based on SO_2 and particulate concentrations, really answered the need. We have had many favorable comments, with a generally favorable response from the public.

AGENCY NO. 26   AGENCY SIZE: 237   INDEX TYPE: $3D_1A$

In general, the public is not technically capable of interpreting the index values. Furthermore, combining several pollutant concentrations into one index number does not accurately reflect air quality. As a result, our index reports actual pollutant concentrations with a "low," "medium," and "high" classification scheme which relates the pollutant concentration to its standard.

AGENCY NO. 27   AGENCY SIZE: <10   INDEX TYPE: $3A_3B$

This index is not good for much besides public information. It generally has been accepted well by the public, and the television stations and newspapers report the index daily. The idea of a uniform national index is appealing, but such an index should not be complex (i.e., ORAQI), since smaller agencies would have difficulty handling it.

*NOTE: THESE ARE INTERPRETATIONS BY THE INVESTIGATORS OF VIEWS EXPRESSED BY RESPONDENTS DURING TELEPHONE CONVERSATIONS.

AGENCIES USING INDICES (Cont'd)

AGENCY NO. 28   AGENCY SIZE: 37   INDEX TYPE: $3A_3B$

Our index was initiated to give the public a better idea about the quality of the air. It is calculated by weighting each pollutant concentration differently and then computing the average of the resulting values. The weighting of each pollutant concentration is very resonable in that the values obtained give a low-to-high, good-to-bad scale. However, we have reservations about the averaging operation, because it tends to mask higher pollutant concentrations. Regarding a uniform national index, some cities may not like the idea, because it will "compare" them to other cities, or they may just want to have their own index.

AGENCY NO. 29   AGENCY SIZE: 228   INDEX TYPE: $5B_2B$

Our index has received a favorable response from the public. It was developed by our state agency for use in 12 local air pollution control agencies. Now, our greatest need is for standardized guidelines for the location of monitoring stations.

* NOTE: THESE ARE INTERPRETATIONS BY THE INVESTIGATORS OF VIEWS EXPRESSED BY RESPONDENTS DURING TELEPHONE CONVERSATIONS.

139

AGENCIES NOT USING INDICES

AGENCY NO. 30   AGENCY SIZE: 25

We previously had an index, the Oak Ridge Air Quality Index (ORAQI), which we used for a couple of years. We tried to correlate the index with visibility but found it didn't work. The poor relationship between observed visibility and index values created public confusion, and we had many complaints. We feel that some form of index is needed, however, but it should be one that has meaning to the public -- not one that produces contradictions between index values and perceived pollution levels.

AGENCY NO. 31   AGENCY SIZE: 26

Our agency reports the actual air pollutant concentrations -- carbon monoxide, oxidant, nitrogen dioxide, particulates. These concentrations, along with forecast values for the following day are reported by the newspaper along with the weather summary. A combined index would require us to add the gases and particulates, which does not seem reasonable. We have found it possible to educate the public about the meaning of these four pollutants, and a combined index does not seem necessary.

AGENCY NO. 32   AGENCY SIZE: 53

For our public, use of an air pollution index probably would be confusing. We would rather educate the public to understand the scientific units (i.e., parts per million, micrograms per cubic meter). Although this education process is difficult, we believe that our public is just beginning to understand. In a given city, the decision on whether or not to use an index probably depends on the public involved. This decision probably varies from city to city; any approach is all right so long as the public understands it. In our area, photochemical oxidant is the largest problem, so we report these concentrations, along with a 30-hour oxidant forecast.

*NOTE: THESE ARE INTERPRETATIONS BY THE INVESTIGATORS OF VIEWS EXPRESSED BY RESPONDENTS DURING TELEPHONE CONVERSATIONS.

<u>AGENCIES NOT USING INDICES</u> (Cont'd)

AGENCY NO. 33   AGENCY SIZE: 53

Our agency does not use an index. The concept of
an air pollution index probably is a good one, but
there are not enough studies yet to provide a solid
basis for such an index. If our agency adopts an air
pollution index, we probably will develop one ourselves。
With the telemetered data now available from our
monitoring stations, an index for our agency might be
a good idea.

AGENCY NO. 34   AGENCY SIZE: 11

We considered adopting an air pollution index for
our air pollution control agency, and the Oak Ridge
Air Quality Index (ORAQI) was proposed. Our air pollution control board turned it down, however, because
we didn't have enough staff to compile the index.

AGENCY SIZE: 35   AGENCY SIZE: 21

We have only a very limited air monitoring network.
It provides only one 24-hour high-volume sampler reading
at each of two sites per week. Therefore, we do not
now have enough monitoring data to implement a daily
air pollution index.

AGENCY NO. 36   AGENCY SIZE: 175

In general, indices leave much open to interpretation. The air quality categories used in many
indices don't tell the exact story.

AGENCY NO. 37   AGENCY SIZE: 18

We feel that the index we are currently
formulating for adoption in early 1975 will give a
better representation of environmental conditions
to the public than is possible at present.

AGENCIES NOT USING INDICES (Cont'd)

AGENCY NO. 38   AGENCY SIZE: 87

Although it was suggested several years ago
that the two newspapers begin reporting air pollution
levels, such reporting began only recently. Now
using the daily pollutant concentrations supplied
by our agency, one newspaper reports concentrations
as a percentage of federal standards, while the other
reports the actual concentrations along with the
corresponding federal standard. Because the percentage scheme appears more acceptable, we may
begin reporting our data to the newspapers in
this manner in the future.

AGENCY NO. 39   AGENCY SIZE: 15

We do not now use an air pollution index, but we
have looked into it. Unfortunately, it is difficult
to get an index that everyone can agree upon. We would
use an index if we could find one that is understandable
to all and agreeable to all.

AGENCY NO. 40   AGENCY SIZE: 35

We have been asked many times to implement an
air pollution index. However, since air pollution is
too complex, the general public would not really
understand an air pollution index. We don't believe
it is possible to construct an index that is truly
meaningful and sensible. Any index will inevitably
give values that contradict the public's own ob-
servations and perception, and we don't want to
make something that's misleading. Thus, we give
the public the actual measured data; if they can't
understand it, too bad. If we attempt to reduce
these complex data to some simple index, we're just
kidding ourselves.

*NOTE: THESE ARE INTERPRETATIONS BY THE INVESTIGATORS OF VIEWS EXPRESSED BY RESPONDENTS DURING
TELEPHONE CONVERSATIONS.

AGENCIES NOT USING INDICES (Cont'd)

AGENCY NO. 41   AGENCY SIZE: 15

Ours is not really an index based on air quality; instead, we report an "air pollution potential index" which is based on meteorological conditions (i.e., ventilation) and informs the public whether they should burn or not. We feel it is better to forecast forth-coming conditions than to report yesterday's values. It probably would be a good idea, however, for EPA to come up with a basic index so that we could compare conditions in different cities.

AGENCY NO. 42   AGENCY SIZE: 14

We don't now use an index because our sampling network previously has been too limited. Most indices represent a "non-understandable, non-dimensional number." Everyone seems to use an index, and they all are doing it a bit differently; as a result, the indices are really not interpretable. We might use a stand-ardized index, however, if EPA were to propose one.

AGENCY NO. 43   AGENCY SIZE: 10

We do not now use an air pollution index, because we never have found one that was satisfactory. We would like one that includes particulates and SO_2; it might possibly be beneficial to us.

AGENCY NO. 44   AGENCY SIZE: 76

We do not use an index; we do, however, routinely predict the next day's particulate level. I don't think a combined index really is clear to the public; it can really confuse them. We prefer to encourage them to use the scientific notation -- i.e., ug/m^3. With so many different air quality indices around, "people really can get confused when they move from city to city." We think it would be best to strive to familiarize the general public with "ug/m^3 particulate" for example. They can become familiar with this scien-tific notation just as they have learned to understand wind speed in miles per hour and temperature in degrees. Whenever we report our concentration data, we also list the air quality standards in one column alongside the data.

*NOTE: THESE ARE INTERPRETATIONS BY THE INVESTIGATORS OF VIEWS EXPRESSED BY RESPONDENTS DURING TELEPHONE CONVERSATIONS.

AGENCIES NOT USING INDICES (Cont'd)

AGENCY NO. 45   AGENCY SIZE: 45

We have no routine air monitoring data; thus, there is no way for us to use an index. The data we do collect is primarily for enforcement purposes

AGENCY NO. 46   AGENCY SIZE: 25

An air quality index is a good idea if its meaning can be clearly explained to the public.

AGENCY NO. 47   AGENCY SIZE: 105

Several years ago, in order to maintain good public relations, we were "pushed into" publishing a daily air quality report consisting of a "good," "average," or "poor" ratings. Due to its inherent inadequacies, the system was discontinued about a year ago. If a new index is established, it will not be a combined index since combined indices do not represent true air quality.

AGENCY NO. 48   AGENCY SIZE: 15

Our index was discontinued about a year ago because it did not give a true indication of the air quality. However, we still get requests for it, and are currently considering implementing a new index.

AGENCY NO. 49   AGENCY SIZE: <10

We used an index for a while and received favorable public response, but we had to discontinue it because parts of the media "sensationalized" the higher index values by stating "the index is now at 80 and when it gets to 100 you will have to start worrying." In general, the public must fully understand any index which is used.

---

* **NOTE**: THESE ARE INTERPRETATIONS BY THE INVESTIGATORS OF VIEWS EXPRESSED BY RESPONDENTS DURING TELEPHONE CONVERSATIONS.

APPENDIX D

EXAMPLES OF INDEX DISPLAY AND
DISSEMINATION TECHNIQUES

THE ATLANTA CONSTITUTION, Friday, Dec. 6, 1974

Atlanta

Air Pollution Index....................	.30
Rainfall..............................	.00
Rainfall to Date 1974...............	41.96
Normal Rainfall....................	44.75
High Thursday......................	53
Low Thursday.......................	29
Mean Temperature...................	41
Normal Mean.......................	46
High One Year Ago Friday............	56
Low One Year Ago Friday............	31
Highest Recorded This Date.....	77 (1956)
Lowest Recorded This Date.....	14 (1937)
Winds Friday....	Southeasterly 8-12 m.p.h.
Sunrise Friday...........	7:28 a.m. EST
Sunset Friday..................	5:29 p.m.

Atlanta, Georgia

Baltimore Morning Sun
November 22, 1974

Yesterday's Pollution

Air quality in Baltimore at 2 P.M. yesterday was good, according to the Maryland Department of Health and Mental Hygiene's computerized air monitoring system.

Baltimore, Md.

Washington Star-News

Thursday, January 30, 1975

Air Quality Index

The air quality index in the Washington area from 8 a.m. to 9 a.m. today was 11 for the pollutant sulfer dioxide. Index values between 0-24 indicate good air quality.

THE WASHINGTON POST *Thursday, Jan. 30, 1975*

The Council of Governments' Air Quality Index for yesterday showed the high reading in the Washington area during the 2 to 3 p.m. period was 19 for the pollutant, photochemical oxidants. Index values between 0 and 24 indicate good air quality. When the index exceeds 100 the air becomes hazardous, and persons with lung, heart and eye problems should restrict their activity.

Washington, D.C.

Minnesota

Duluth

POST-BULLETIN, ROCHESTER, MINN., Thursday, August 1, 1974__

24-Hour Air Pollution Index: 32

The Air Pollution Index is an average degree of air pollution for a 24-hour period ending 10 a.m. for Rochester. The index, compiled at the Public Health Center, 415 4th St. SE, combines measurements and estimates of the levels of three major air pollutants here: sulpher dioxide, carbon monoxide and particulates (dust). A reading between 0-25 is "good"; between 26-100 is "satisfactory"; between 101-155 is "unsatisfactory" and between 156-200 is "unsatisfactory"

Rochester

146

New York

Buffalo Evening News
11/26/74

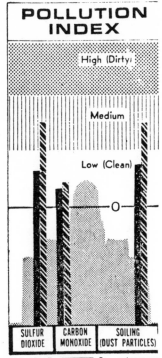

POLLUTION INDEX

High (Dirty)

Medium

Low (Clean)

0

| SULFUR DIOXIDE | CARBON MONOXIDE | SOILING (DUST PARTICLES) |

24-Hr. Reading ▓▓▓▓ Forecast ▨▨▨

Today's Buffalo reading

Sulfur Dioxide ....0.01   Low
Carbon Monoxide ....2.4   Low
Soling (Dust) ....0.3   Low

Today's Niagara Falls reading:

Sulfur Dioxide .... 0.03   Medium
Carbon Monoxide ....2.9   Low
Soling (Dust) ....0.3   Low

The readings represent average air, pollution levels for a 24-hour period ending at midnight as measured at the continuous air monitoring stations.

The State Department of Environmental Conservation's Division of Air Resources provides this key to interpreting the readings:

Sulfur Dioxide—(In parts per million); low less than 03; medium .03 to .08; high greater than .08.

Carbon Monoxide—(In parts per million): low less than 5.9; medium, 5.0 to 15.0; high greater than 15.0.

Soiling—(In reflectant units of dirt shade): low, less than 0.4; medium, 0.4 to 0.7; high, greater than 0.7.

Buffalo

Knickerbocker News
11/26/74
Albany, N.Y.

Air Pollution

	Today	Rating
Sulfur Dioxide	0.02	Low
Carbon Monoxide	3.2	Low
Soiling	0.2	Low

Albany

Today's pollution index:
31 (very good).

Akron

AIR POLLUTION INDEX
Toledo's air pollution index for the 24-hour period which ended at 8 a.m. today was 42, indicating air of very good quality. The major air pollutant during the period was ozone.

Toledo

Tomorrow's pollution forecast: 170 to 190 (extremely poor).

Cleveland

The Cincinnati Post, Friday, Nov. 22, 1974

Pollution index

The air pollution index at 9 a.m. was 42, which is rated very good, better than the clean air standard. At 4 p.m. yesterday the index stood at 45, which is rated very good, better than the clean air standard.

The discomfort level for pollutants is 200; the warning level 300, and the emergency level 400—when all industry and autos, the main pollutors of air, would be ordered by the governor to come to a halt.

The Cincinnati Enquirer
November 22, 1974

Weather

Mostly sunny today, high upper 40s. Variable cloudiness tonight and Saturday. Low tonight, upper 30s. High Saturday around 60. Air Pollution Index, 45, very good.

Details, Map on Page 16

Cincinnati

Pennsylvania

The Pittsburgh Press
December 6, 1974

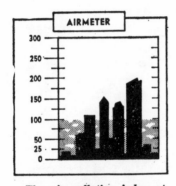

The air pollution index at 10 a. m. today in downtown Pittsburgh was 98.

This is 63 points over the maximum level established by county authorities as satisfactory quality air.

Other readings in the county today include: Bellevue, 80; Glassport, 82; Hazelwood No. 1, 92; Hazelwood No. 2, 63; Liberty Borough, 87, and Logan's Ferry Heights, 61.

Pittsburgh

Tuesday, Aug. 13, 1974   Philadelphia Inquirer

AIR QUALITY
Monday's Pollution Index: 5.
The Air Pollution Index, compiled by the Philadelphia Air Management Services, is a 1 (clean) to 10 (dirty) scale based on measurements of sulphur dioxide and particulate matter in the air in the last five years. Since concentrations have dropped in recent years, the daily reading usually is in the lower half of the scale.

Philadelphia

APPENDIX E

STANDARDIZED URBAN AIR QUALITY INDEX

The Standardized Urban Air Quality Index (SUAQI) presented here is based on the results of this study and the uniform index criteria identified during this investigation (Chapter VI, Section 4). SUAQI is a type $5B_2B$ index. However, it could equally well have been a type $5D_2B$ index. Since it is based on the best available current information, this basic structure represents one feasible form that a future SUAQI might take.

Besides selecting the index structure, there are many other problems which must be confronted by jurisdictions adopting a uniform index. Some of these relate to the governmental procedures required for the adoption of an index, some relate to the siting of monitoring stations, and some relate to the manner by which the index is reported to the public. These problems are not dealt with here. However, as discussed in Chapter VIII, it is hoped a document will be completed which provides detailed procedures for adoption and implementation of a uniform index.

The following discussion gives the basic structure of SUAQI according to the order of the index classification system (Chapter VI, Section 2).

Number of Pollutants. Due to the seasonal variation in pollutant concentrations and the emphasis on different pollutants in different parts of the country, SUAQI incorporates all of the most common air pollutants. However, SUAQI does not include pollutants for which standards do not exist. Since uniform NAAQS have been adopted by the Federal Government, the five pollutants covered by these standards were chosen -- carbon monoxide, sulfur dioxide, suspended particulate matter, nitrogen oxides, and photochemical oxidants. Because of its structure, if the number of NAAQS pollutants changes in the future, the SUAQI will be able to accommodate such changes without modifying its basic form.

Calculation Method. A linear function with nonconstant coefficients (segmented linear function) is used. The SUAQI breakpoints (Table E-1) are based on the NAAQS and Federal Episode Criteria. A plot of each set of values (pollutant concentration, K) gives a SUAQI function for each of the five pollutants (Figures E-1 to E-6). If new NAAQS are adopted in the future, a new SUAQI function can easily be drawn to accommodate it.

Mode. Inasmuch as SUAQI is based on the NAAQS and episode criteria, which do not include any standards for the combinations of pollutants (except product SO_2-COH), the index can either be an individual or maximum type. The maximum type has been selected, since it reports only one pollutant index (the highest one), thus preventing the public from becoming overwhelmed with too many index values. However, in some cases it may be desirable to report an index value for all pollutants which equal or exceed the Primary NAAQS. The maximum mode also enables the greatest utilization of existing monitoring equipment, which in most cities is directed at the city's problem pollutants.

Descriptor Categories. Inasmuch as the index calculation is based on the NAAQS and Federal Episode Criteria, it is logical that the descriptor categories be based on these same standards. As a result of the findings of this study, three of four categories are used to describe pollution levels. The four SUAQI categories and their descriptor words are shown in Table E-2. "Hazardous" is used to describe air pollution levels at and above the Alert level to prevent confusion when pollution levels exceed this level but an Alert is not called.

152

TABLE E-1

BREAKPOINTS FOR SUAQI

	K	CO ppm	SO_2 ppm	PM $\mu g/m^3$	$SO_2 \times PM$ $(\mu g/m^3)^2$	ppm	Ox ppm
Averaging Time (hours)	NA	8	24	24	24	1	1
Secondary NAAQS	50	a/	b/	150	b/	b/	a/
Primary NAAQS	100	9	0.14	260	b/	b/	0.08
Alert	200	15	0.3	375	65,000	0.6	0.10
Warning	300	30	0.6	625	261,000	1.2	0.40
Emergency	400	40	0.8	875	393,000	1.6	0.50
Significant Harm	500	50	1.0	1,000	490,000	2.0	0.60

a/ Secondary same as Primary NAAQS

b/ No NAAQS for this averaging time

153

TABLE E-2

SUAQI DESCRIPTOR CATEGORIES

SUAQI	Standard	Descriptor
0- 50	At or below Secondary NAAQS	Good
51-100	At or below Primary NAAQS	Satisfactory
101-199	Above Primary NAAQS	Unhealthful
200-299	Alert	
300-399	Warning	
400-499	Emergency	Hazardous
500 and greater	Significant Harm	

154

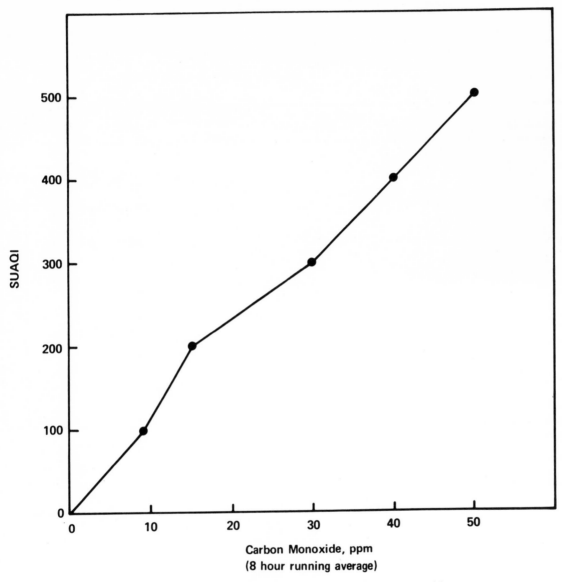

Figure E-1. SUAQI function for carbon monoxide

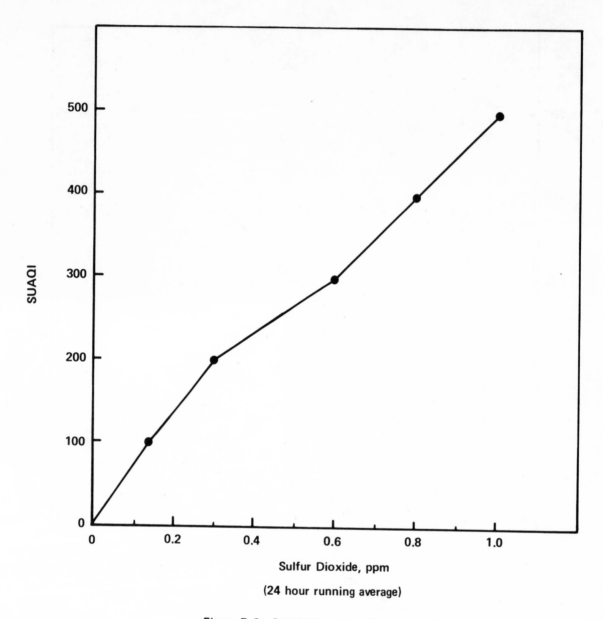

Figure E-2. SUAQI function for sulfur dioxide

156

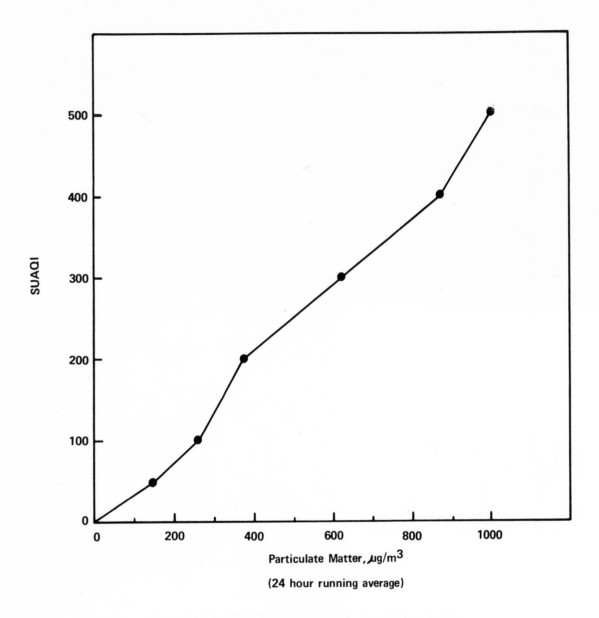

Figure E-3. SUAQI function for particulate matter.

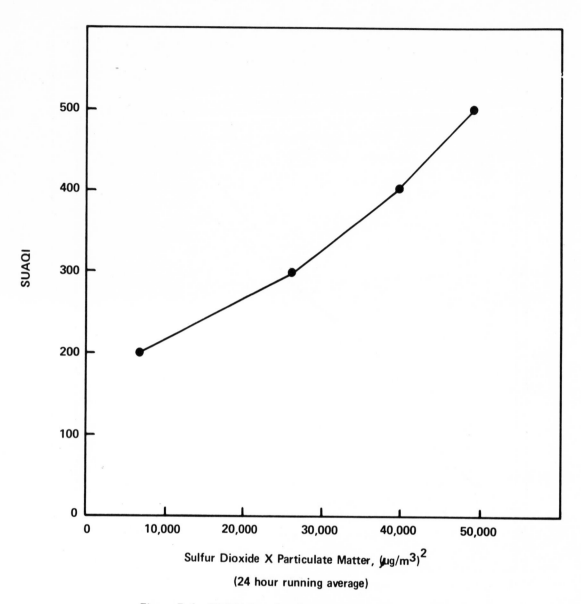

Figure E-4. SUAQI function for the product of sulfur dioxide
and particulate matter

158

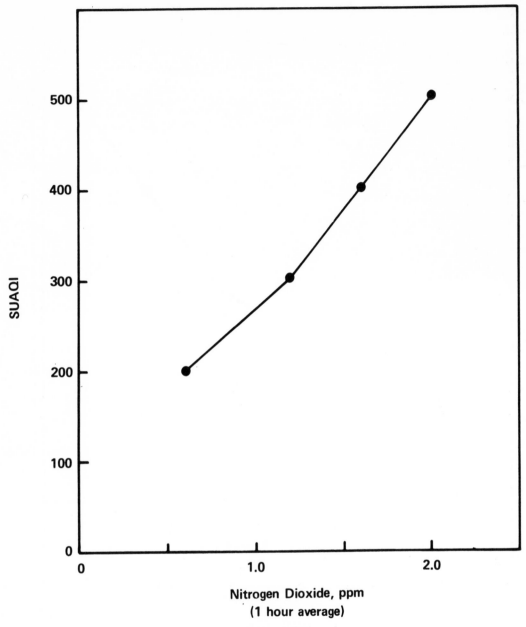

Figure E–5. SUAQI function for nitrogen dioxide

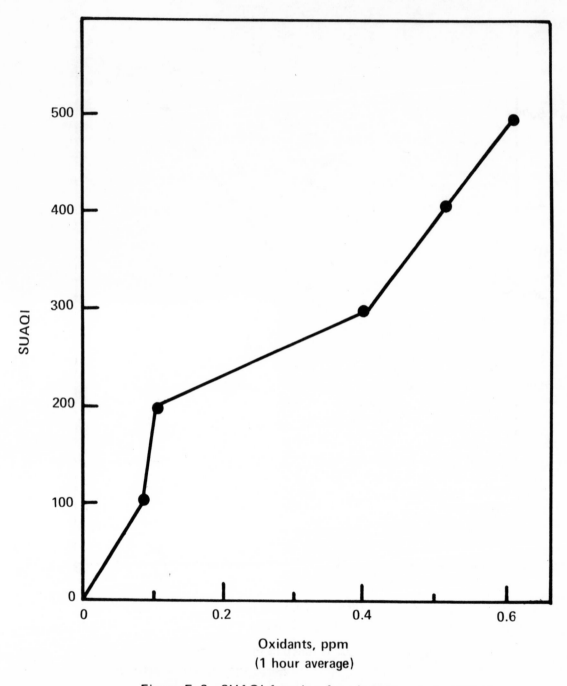

Figure E-6. SUAQI function for photochemical oxidants

APPENDIX F

PRIMARY STANDARDS INDEX

The Primary Standards Index (PSI) is a second example of a possible standardized index and is derived from the recently proposed Common Air Quality Reporting Format.[23/] PSI was developed after reviewing the comments received from some Federal, State, and local air pollution control officials on SUAQI (Appendix E), and it reflects the opinion of some reviewers that a standardized index should be simpler than SUAQI and relate only to the Primary NAAQS and their associated health effects. Thus, PSI has only two descriptor categories (whereas SUAQI has four), and it relates directly to health effects by reporting the adverse effects associated with pollutant levels exceeding the Primary NAAQS.

PSI is a type $4C_2B$ index and thus has the same structure as SUAQI ($5B_2B$), except PSI uses a linear (instead of a segmented linear) calculation method. The following discussion outlines the basic structure of PSI, according to the order of the index classification system (Chapter VI, Section 2). Other details of the index (implementation procedure, monitoring siting, and format) should be covered in the Index Monitoring Guidelines document discussed in Chapter VIII.

Number of Pollutants. PSI includes all pollutants for which a Primary NAAQS exists (presently four): carbon

161

monoxide, sulfur dioxide, particulate matter, and oxidants.
Because PSI gives separate index values for each pollutant
an agency can select which of the four pollutants it wishes
to include in a PSI report.

Calculation Method. PSI is a linear function with a
constant coefficient of 100. Thus, it is a "percent-of-
standards index," which, for each pollutant, gives the
percent of the corresponding Primary NAAQS (Table F-1).
The PSI equation is given as:

$$PSI_i = K \, c_i$$

where, $K = 100/C_{s_i}$; c_i is the concentration of pollutant
$\underline{i}$; and C_{s_i} is the NAAQS for pollutant $\underline{i}$. Combining these
definitions:

$$PSI_i = 100 \, \frac{c_i}{C_{s_i}}$$

Using this equation, PSI values for new pollutants are
easily accommodated in the total index structure.

Mode. In reporting PSI, either the individual index
values or the maximum value can be used. Alternatively,
one can report only those values which exceed the

TABLE F-1

POSSIBLE ADVERSE HEALTH EFFECTS FOR PSI GREATER THAN 100

Pollutant	Averaging Time	Primary NAAQS	Explaination Given when PSI > 100 (Unhealthy)
CO	8	9 ppm	•Impaired exercise tolerance in persons with cardio-vascular disease
SO_2	1	35 ppm	•Decreased physical performance in normal adults
	24	0.14 ppm	•Increased hospital admissions for respiratory illness
			•Aggravation of asthma and cardiorespiratory symptoms in elderly patients with related illness
TSP	24	260 $\mu g/m^3$	•Aggravation of chronic lung disease and asthma
			•Aggravation of cardiorespiratory disease symptoms in elderly patients with heart or chronic lung disease
			•Increased cough, chest discomfort, and restricted activity
Ox	1	0.08 ppm	•Aggravation of chronic lung disease and asthma
			•Irritation of the respiratory tract in healthy adults
			•Decreased visualy acuity; eye irritation
			•Decreased cardiopulmonary reserve in healthy subjects

Primary NAAQS. Such an approach gives an agency maximum
flexibility in using its existing monitoring network and
data to compute the index.

Descriptor Categories. Since PSI is based only on
one "breakpoint', the Primary NAAQS, only two descriptor
categories are needed:

TABLE F-2

PSI DESCRIPTOR CATEGORIES

PSI	Standard	Descriptor
0-100	At or below Primary NAAQS	Satisfactory
>100	Above Primary NAAQS	Unhealthful

In addition to these descriptor words, the associated
possible adverse health effects listed in Table F-1 are
reported for those pollutants exceeding the Primary NAAQS
(PSI >100). In the cases when the Federal Episode Criteria
apply (Table 2, page 20), the air quality may still be
termed "unhealthful" and used in conjunction with the Alert,
Warning, and Emergency stage designations.